D1134431

# JOHNNIE WALKER'S
# BURNS SUPPER
# COMPANION

*To*

*J. F. T. THOMSON*
*whose love of Burns and*
*dedication to the Burns movement*
*will long be remembered.*

JOHNNIE WALKER'S

# BURNS SUPPER COMPANION

HUGH DOUGLAS

ALLOWAY PUBLISHING, AYR.

© Hugh Douglas, 1981

First Published in 1981
Second Edition 1983
by Alloway Publishing Ltd.,
Ayr.

Printed in Scotland.
by Walker & Connell Ltd.,
Hastings Square, Darvel,
Ayrshire.

Line Drawings by
Stephen Hunter

ISBN 0 907526 01 2

# CONTENTS

Why a Burns Supper? . . . . . . . . . . .9

Could I really run a Burns Supper? .21

Help! Where do I Start?. . . . . . . . .24

The Chairman . . . . . . . . . . . . . . . .36

Enter the Haggis . . . . . . . . . . . . . .42

Interlude. . . . . . . . . . . . . . . . . . . .50

Immortal Memory. . . . . . . . . . . . .53

The Other Speeches. . . . . . . . . . . .79

Sangs and Clatter. . . . . . . . . . . . . .85

Time to Skail. . . . . . . . . . . . . . . . .89

The Morn's Morning . . . . . . . . . . .93

The Apt Quotation . . . . . . . . . . . .98

The Dram . . . . . . . . . . . . . . . . . .106

List of Suppliers . . . . . . . . . . . . .110

Engraved by W. Holl from the original by Nasmyth.

# Foreword

Every year, thousands of unsuspecting souls who have scarcely read a line of Robert Burns's poetry in their lives are invited to address a Burns Supper, either to propose the Immortal Memory of Burns, to toast the Lassies, or even to address the haggis. Often the organiser is unable to offer them much help because he too is inexperienced in the art of honouring Scotland's National Bard.

Johnnie Walker's Burns Supper Companion is a lifeline for all of them.

To strangers the mysteries of the 25th January may seem peculiar, even comic. To Scots the whole business of Burns Night is deadly serious. They recognise the Burns Supper as a highly formalised, even ritualistic celebration which follows the same pattern in Adelaide as in Alloway, where Burns was born. Within that basic structure, however, there is infinite variety to make each celebration a unique tribute to the poetic genius of Scotland's favourite son. This makes it the more difficult for the uninitiated to arrange a Burns Supper — should he stray from the set pattern he will never be forgiven by Burnsians : but should he arrange a Supper which does not add to the Burns dimension woe betide him also.

I would like to thank Allan Ramsay and Drew Stevenson for their generous help and advice. F. Marian McNeill's haggis recipe comes from her book *The Scots Kitchen* and I am grateful to the publishers, Blackie and Son for permission to reproduce it. The Burns Federation, which does so much fine work to foster interest in Burns, has given me help on a number of points and I thank its Hon. Secretary, Mr. J.F.T. Thomson and his staff at the Dick Institute, Kilmarnock. I have tried to unlock the door to the mysteries of Burns Night and to help those who are organising the evening, proposing a toast, or merely attending as a guest. I hope the book will add to the enjoyment of what has virtually become Scotland's National Day.

Hugh Douglas
1981

# WHY A BURNS SUPPER?

O OUT into the main street of Ayr, Aberdeen, Arbroath or Aberdour and stop a hundred people, ask them, "When is Scotland's National Day?" and the majority will reply, "The 25th of January." Patron Saint, Saint Andrew and his day on the 30th November pass virtually unnoticed, but Scots, not just in Scotland but in every part of the world, flock to eat haggis, to hear their own tongue spoken, to drink not a few drams of whisky, and to honour their country's greatest son.

Who is the greatest Scot of all time? Ask the same people in Ayr, Aberdeen, Arbroath or Aberdour; stop another hundred in Airdrie, Ardrossan and Auchtermuchty and ask them too, and the answer will come back without hesitation — Robert Burns. Of course there are other contenders for the title, the greatest Scot, especially Robert the Bruce, but Burns wins the poll every time because he is a man who not only gave a great legacy of poetry, but has grown in stature as a man year by year since his death nearly two centuries ago.

And to begin to appreciate why hundreds of thousands of Scots round the world, and a considerable number of non-Scots in places as far apart as Moscow and Tokyo, celebrates Burns's birthday on the 25th January it is necessary to understand something of Robert Burns and what he achieved in the 37 brief years which he was given to do his work.

Robert Burns was born on...well, like so many

of the facts about his life he told us himself...

Our monarch's hindmost year but ane*
Was five-and-twenty days begun,
'Twas then a blast o' Janwar' Win',
    Blew hansel* in on Robin.                    * first gift

*1759, last year of George II's reign.

He told us a lot more in this poem — that he
would be a roving lad with an eye for the girls for
example — and he summed up his own life better
than anyone else could have done...

He'll hae misfortunes great and sma'
But ay a heart aboon them a';
He'll be a credit till us a',
    We'll a' be proud o' Robin!

From an early age Robert must have known
that life was going to be hard. Outwardly the
signs were promising enough for his parents
William and Agnes Burnes* lived in a little house
at Alloway which compared well with the
conditions in which other folk of their kind lived.
William had built the house himself and was
running a market garden, which appeared to do
well. But he had ambitions for himself and for
his children: he wanted to be a farmer so he took
a lease of Mount Oliphant farm a few miles inland

from Alloway, and he clubbed together with other farming folk to hire a schoolmaster to teach his children and theirs.

As Robert Burns grew up there was little time for formal education — a few weeks at Dalrymple, a spell at Kirkoswald, and a short stay with his old tutor in Ayr until he had to hurry back to help with the harvest. Soon he and his brother Gilbert were the chief workers on their father's farm, and it was at this time that Robert developed the heart condition which was to claim his life. Robert Burns did not die of excessive drinking; he died from the effects of overwork in his youth.

Mount Oliphant did not prosper in spite of all the hard work the family put into it. Neither did Lochlea at Tarbolton, to which they moved in 1777, and where a prolonged legal wrangle over the lease was added to all the other worries. Robert managed to lead a full life during the Lochlea years, and even to wring some enjoyment from it. He joined with friends to found the Bachelors' debating club in Tarbolton, to learn to dance, to argue earnestly with every person in the parish who was prepared to discuss the issues of the day with him and, of course, to meet girls and begin to earn the reputation as a womaniser which has endured for two hundred years.

It was when he was working in the harvest field beside a girl called Nelly Kirkpatrick that he first "committted the sin of verse" by composing a little song to her...

*Robert was the first of the family to drop the 'e'.

O once I lov'd a bonnie lass,
An' aye I love her still,
An' whilst that virtue warms my breast
I'll love my handsome Nell.

From then on he never stopped writing verse
or wooing bonnie lassies, and both drew him into
conflict with authority, his elders and the Kirk.

His father died in 1784, at the end of the
distressing lawsuit over the tenancy of Lochlea,
and Robert was left as head of the family. It was
a heavy burden for a young man just turned
twenty-five, but he faced up to it squarely and
even after success as a poet took him away from
the family he supported them to the extent of
depriving himself of an easy life.

The Burns family moved to Mossgiel farm at
Mauchline, and it was there that Robert began to
catch the public's eye, first as the father of
servant girl Lizzie Paton's illegitimate daughter,
then as a rebel against the narrowness and
hypocrisy in the Church, and thirdly as a poet
with a sharp pen to satirize those faults within
the Kirk and the faults in his fellow humans. Next
Jean Armour was pregnant and Burns was being
hotly pursued by the Reverend William "Daddy"
Auld, the Mauchline minister and by Jean's
father, so that he thought seriously of emigrating
to Jamaica to escape.

That was until July 1786, when a book
containing three dozen of his poems appeared.
John Wilson, the Kilmarnock printer, produced
612 copies of *Poems Chiefly in the Scottish
Dialect*, and within weeks the whole countryside was aflame with interest in it. The rich
clamoured for it: so did servant men and girls

who could ill afford three shillings to buy a copy, and soon Burns's fame had spread to Edinburgh but by that time the book was sold out.

In the Autumn of 1786 Burns went to Edinburgh to arrange for a second book to be published and there he spent a winter in the dizzy world of the capital's society. By the following spring he was glad to escape to the Borders to make the first of three tours to see other parts of the country. His second and third tours took him to the West Highlands, the Highlands and Perthshire, Stirlingshire, Clackmannan and Fife, but this first one was made with a purpose — to view Ellisland, a farm on which he had been offered a lease, near Dumfries. Burns was beginning to feel he must settle down.

He went to Mauchline briefly and again met Jean Armour who had borne him twins during his absence, and who as a result of his return was soon pregnant again. To his dying day Burns had an eye for a girl, and too often his affairs ended in the same way. Rumour said that "Highland Mary" Campbell died bearing his child (but that seems unlikely), Meg Cameron and Jenny Clow, servant girls in Edinburgh, and Anna Park in Dumfries all bore him children, but Agnes Maclehose, Clarinda of his passionate affair in Edinburgh during the winter of 1787-88, kept him at arm's length although she did inspire one of his loveliest songs, *Ae Fond Kiss.*

Burns took the Ellisland lease - and like his father had to build a home on it for his wife and family, for he had at last married Jean Armour. He had been too generous to his family to keep Mossgiel afloat and now hadn't enough capital to set himself up in Ellisland and he soon had to take a job with the Excise service to eke out the bare living the farm could yield. He rode two hundred miles a week carrying out his Excise duties and still managed to tame the dour earth of Ellisland by the river Nith, but it told on his health and he was glad to be rid of the farm and to move into Dumfries to work solely for the Excise

He worked hard; he did well; but these were difficult times and, since an Exciseman's earnings depended on imports, Burns's income dropped during the French wars. But he was a man with prospects, living in a fine big sandstone house, and highly thought of by people who mattered.

However, his health was worsening and he often became depressed and ill. As a result he quarrelled with some of his best friends and nearly fell foul of his Excise masters in Edinburgh. It has often been suggested that his loyalty was in question at the time of the French Revolution, but this is disproved by the fact that he joined the volunteer regiment which was raised to fend off the feared invasion.

In 1796 he was being dunned by the tailor for payment of the cost of his uniform and this preyed on his mind. He became ill, and as his health worsened his doctor sent him to Brow on the Solway Firth for sea-bathing which, far from curing him, hastened his death. He returned to Dumfries to the dunning tailor, to Jean who was on the point of giving him another child - and to certain death. On 21st July, 1796, he died, still fearful for his family's future.

His fears were unfounded for at once his friends raised a fund for Jean and the children, and then another book of his poems was published, and from that moment the family never was in want. What is heartwarming is not that people rallied to give a few shillings or pounds to his widow, but that his stature as a poet grew and has continued to grow ever since his death.

He wrote such a variety of poems, from brilliant, incisive satires against hypocrisy around him to his matchless narrative poem *Tam O' Shanter* He wrote poems sympathetic to nature all round him, yet summing all man's inhumanity to man and the consequent suffering. When he wrote of the mouse's suffering he was writing about any man's grief...

> The best laid schemes o' Mice and Men,
>     Gang aft agley,*        * often go wrong
> An' lea'e us nought but grief an' pain,
>     For promis'd joy.

On mankind's own frailties Burns's thoughts ran deep, but he expressed them in language which was both beautiful and simple...

> The heart ay's the part ay'
> That makes us right or wrang.

He brought decency into life where there had been very little before. He raised hope where it had been dashed by life. He taught self respect where there was little encouragement for such a virtue. And as if that weren't enough, he rescued the Scottish tongue at a time when strong forces were anglicizing it, and he gave the Scottish people renewed sense of nationhood at the moment when the country was fast becoming mere North Britain, an appendage of England. Had Burns not paved the way Walter Scott could not have helped the Scottish people to discover the beauty of their homeland.

Perhaps Burns is best remembered for his songs — over 300 of them expressing every emotion from loyalty to love, and for every occasion from meeting to parting. Many of Burns's songs live on, but it is his *Auld Lang Syne* which has become an international song of brotherhood and has been translated into many languages to be sung at the moment of parting. To the Scot *Auld Lang Syne* takes on a deep meaning, reminding him of a way of life that has gone and of the places which mean so much. As he sings the verses he remembers his own braes and his own burns, but he is not sad for *Auld Lang Syne* is not meant to be a sad song. It ends on a note of happiness and hope, offering the hand of friendship and the promise of future convivial evenings together . . .

> And there's a hand, my trusty fiere!*   *Companion
> And gie's a hand o' thine!

And we'll tak a right gude-willy waught,*          * drink
   For auld lang syne.

For that one song alone Burns deserves immortality.

With that background it is small wonder that people who knew Burns realised that his death had robbed them of an understanding friend, and that within a few years a movement to honour his memory had arisen. The Burns Cult, centred on the Burns Supper, was a spontaneous act of appreciation, a response by friends, and that is how it has remained ever since.

On the Poet's birthday in 1801, the *Air Advertiser* reported that " a number of non-commisioned officers and privates of the Argyll Militia went out from Ayr to visit the Cottage (at Alloway), attended by the band of the Regiment, who played a number of appropriate airs." As the Cottage was let out as an inn at this time they were no doubt welcomed for their bar custom as much as for their music.

That same year the first Burns Club was set up at Greenock and the honour of organising the first Burns Supper goes jointly to Greenock and to a group of the Bard's friends at Ayr who met at Alloway in January 1802, and sat down to "a comfortable dinner, of which sheep's head and haggis formed an interesting part". It is the first mention of the haggis which is now an inescapable part of every Burns Anniversary dinner, and which is regarded by many as Burns's staple diet. Burns may not have lived on "skinking ware that jaups in luggies", but he certainly did not eat haggis every day either!

The second Burns Club was instituted at Paisley in 1805 with the town's weaver poet Robert Tannahill as its first secretary, and today the Greenock Club is known as the Mother Club and Paisley as the Daughter Club. Hard on the heels of these clubs followed the reinterment of the Poet's body in a new and grander grave at St. Michael's Church, in Dumfries, under a splendid marble tomb. A lofty classical-pillared Monument was built at Alloway about the same time.

A Burns Festival at Alloway in 1844 was just a rehearsal for the birth centenary commemoration in 1859 when close on 900 celebrations were reported from all parts of the world. The Burns Cult had caught fire and a Burns Federation was set up in Kilmarnock in 1885 to co-ordinate the work of the many Burns Clubs and to enable the Burns movement to encourage the arts of Scotland both at home and beyond the Border.

Year by year the Cult has grown, but one feature of it remains stable — the Burns Supper or Anniversary Dinner. It is impossible to say how many Burns Suppers take place each year, for those organised by societies within the Federation are only a tiny part of the January celebrations.. Other dinners take place in village halls sponsored by women's organisations, in works canteens, arranged by trade union groups, in Russian universities, promoted by Soviet Burnsians, even in aeroplanes, arranged and attended by Burnsians of an international turn of mind.

The range in quality of Burns celebrations is as broad as the range of venues, but Burns would not complain about that. He was an individualist and would abhor the idea of a "standard" Burns Supper, but he would "birl" in his marble mausoleum at the thought of some of the things that are done in his name on Burns Night.

Immortal Memories sometime reflect little credit on the speaker or on Burns, although they are usually well meant. It was *Punch* which remarked on the 1844 Festival that "Scotland is tremendously earnest in all that relates to Burns: earnest alike in her gratitude and her penitence". Earnestness is no excuse for "dreich" speeches, and while the serious side of Burns must be put over, too often earnestness breaks through to dull the mind to Burns or to anything else. The right Burns Supper should send every participant away determined to take down his book of Burns's poems (usually on shelf beside the Bible, as highly thought of and as seldom read) and read it in the morning.

The Burns Supper should have a serious side, though. It is a national celebration if not officially a national day and it is time when every Scot takes stock of himself, of his way of life, and of his fellow-man. It is excellent therapy for any man or for any nation, and so it must be a good thing.

There must be few nations who have been gifted with a genius of the common people as Scotland has been, and it is to Scotland's credit that she should go on year after year expressing her gratitude for his work.

# COULD I REALLY RUN A BURNS SUPPER?

F COURSE you could organise a Burns Supper — But don't if you can persuade somebody else to do it! At most Anniversary Dinners there's plenty of sympathy for the young singer who is showing nerves or for the speaker whose look tells that he is willing the last trump to sound before it is time for him to propose his toast.

Not a thought comes the way of the man or woman who has spent up to a year arranging everything so that the evening will pass so smoothly that no one notices his or her presence. Not a thought, that is, unless something goes wrong. The secretary is the only person who doesn't enjoy the haggis because he is too busy trying to catch the head waiter's eye to make sure he has brought dressing for the vegetarian top table guest's salad. The secretary is the only one who doesn't hear a note of *Ae Fond Kiss* because he is transfixed by a gimlet-eyed guest who thinks he hasn't been allocated as good a place at the table as he thinks he deserves. The secretary is the one man who staggers home exhausted.

Who would be a secretary to organise anything? Who would be a secretary to arrange a club's Burns Supper?

It is unfair to push the whole job of arranging the Anniversary Dinner on to one person, and most larger clubs appreciate this and set up a sub-committee to share the enormous task. Smaller clubs, and organisations who hold a Burns Supper as part of a full social programme, tend to leave the organisation to the secretary or at most to a group of two or three people.

If you are asked to take on the job of arranging the Burns Supper, especially if you have never done it before, it is only reasonable to ask a small sub-committee to help. This means that you will have wider experience than your own to draw on, and on the night, there will be others to take care of the table plan while you devote yourself to looking after the top table guests and general arrangements.

Fortunately the Burns movement is a close and friendly one, so wherever you are there will be a pool of deeper knowledge than your own to call on. Don't hesitate to ask for help — every Burns Supper organiser has to start somewhere and he has enough memories of his own near-disasters in his early days to be sympathetic towards yours. Contact the Secretary or Chairman of your local Burns Club if you require guidance on procedure or even help to find speakers. And if you are unable to solve your problem through the local Club, then get in touch with the Burns Federation headquarters at the Dick Institute in Kilmarnock and seek their help. The Federation exists to ensure that Robert Burns is well served by every function connected with him, and they will do their utmost to ensure that yours maintains the high standard they demand for member clubs.

Organising a Burns Supper, even with the help of a committee, is not easy, but it is rewarding when you hear directly from guests who have attended. or better still, through the Burns Club grapevine, that yours was the best anniversary celebrations in the district, and all the other clubs are after your speakers for their dinners next year.

If you feel equal to the task, read on.

# HELP! WHERE DO I START?

ON'T THINK too hard about where to start planning the event — just plunge in like a swimmer bound for the other side of the Channel and keep going. Where to start planning your Anniversary Dinner is not half as important as when to start. If you are reading this on the 26th January, then it is not a minute too soon to begin work — Burns Night is a mere 364 days away (unless this is a leap year, in which case you have an extra 24 hours).

The best venues, like the best speakers and entertainers, are often booked a full year or more ahead, and it is quite usual for a secretary before he leaves at the end of a Supper, to ask the manager to pencil in a date for next year's event. A good principle to follow is that the better the place or speaker, the further ahead you have to book.

However, before starting to track down a venue it is important to check that your chosen date does not clash with another local society's Dinner, and this is not as formidable a task as it sounds, since the Burnsian grapevine works fast and efficiently. One club secretary will probably be able to give you the dates of all major Burns Night events planned in the district for the following year.

Often clubs have a set date which they adhere to year by year, many avoiding the 25th January itself because that is a date on which certain important Suppers take place. Instead they choose a set date or day each year — say, the 26th

January, or the Friday preceeding the 25th. Some even hold their Dinner as much as a fortnight before or after the 25th, so that they can have a better choice of speakers and local dignitaries, and newspapers will be more likely to have a reporter available.

The important thing is to try to settle on a convenient date and, having established it, to stick to it each year. That way it will quickly find its way into the local Burnsian diary of events as your date and no one will arrange another event to clash with it.

## FINDING A VENUE

With the date chosen (and if this is the club's first Burns Supper, several alternatives in reserve), having decided how many people are likely to attend, and how elaborate a menu you want, it is time to start making arrangements. The first thing to be done is to make a file to hold notes of all meetings held to discuss arrangements and copies of all letters sent out or received in connection with the event. Near the date of the Dinner you should keep this file close to the telephone so that you can refer to the relevant papers when people ring up with queries or problems. The organised organiser is always several moves ahead of the man who keeps notes on the back of an old envelope in his inside coat pocket! With your file you should go round all suitable hotels, restaurants and banqueting suites which cater for such functions. Never drop in casually or make your arrangements as you leave after a meal sometime, and you certainly should never do it all by telephone. Make an appointment in advance and set aside some time to discuss everything in detail. If the manager (or banqueting manager) gives the impression that he cannot spare the time to talk to you now, then the chances are that you will see very little of him on The Night. In the same way, if you rush into his office and out again, he will feel that you are not bringing to his establishment a prestigious function which will make him the envy of every other caterer in the town.

Tell him everything — explain what sort of Anniversary Dinner it is to be (formal, with very important speakers and probably Burns Federation representatives present, or a friendly informal club get-together). Give him details of your speakers and entertainers, and of the sort of meal you are looking for. The more he knows the better he can tailor his service to your needs.

Ask to see the room, the reception facilities for your principal guests, pre-dinner bar facilities, parking space — the lot. Make sure that the room is large enough for the top table guests to walk in procession to table, and that there is room for the haggis ceremonies. A Burns Supper is not like any other dinner: the entertainment lasts a long time and guests need space to set their chairs back an inch or two and relax during it. If a room can take 100 diners for a formal dinner, then 80 will be enough for a Burns Night celebration.

## THE BILL OF FARE

Most catering establishments worthy of the name have plenty of experience in running Burns Suppers, and certainly there are advantages in going to one which is practised in the art of honouring Burns. Apart from anything else, it saves a lot of explaining how you want things done!

These will have standard Burns Night bills of fare* to show you. Haggis will be the focal point of this, but you will have to decide whether it is to be the main course or merely a subsidiary one. It is good to see haggis as the principal dish of the evening, but I confess that this view can be tempered by attending three Burns Suppers on successive nights! On the whole people prefer something less rich as the main course, so it is a good idea to test the opinion of a few members of the society in advance on this question.

Apart from haggis the bill of fare may comprise whatever you think your guests will enjoy. Soup is always popular as the first course and it is an appropriate one since soup has always been an important part of the traditional Scottish farm kitchen. Cock-a-Leekie (chicken and leek soup), Scotch Broth (barley broth) or Bawd Bree (hare soup) are the most popular, but more often one finds Tomato soup (from a tin or packet) on the bill of fare. This is the one meal of the year in which soup should be plain and home-made and it is unforgivable to serve tinned soup.

If haggis is to be the main course then a fish dish, probably salmon, can be served. Herring is more appropriate but it is difficult to get a caterer to serve it these days. Many Clubs have their own traditions as at Alloa where the Club, which began life as Alloa Tripe Club, always serve tripe

*bill of fare is preferable to menu since Burns used the term in To a Haggis.

27

and onions instead of fish.

Then follows the Haggis, the highlight of the evening's fare, with all the usual cermonial (see chapter 6) and served with champit tatties (mashed potatoes) and bashed neeps (mashed turnip or, in England, swede). The potato and turnip sometimes are mashed together with seasoning and butter to form a traditional Orkney dish called Clapshaw. It is a great pity that this is not more often served at home in Scotland nowadays for it is a delicious way of serving the vegetables. The two vegetables combine to form a delicately tasting, rich accompaniment to meat which is quite different from the individual taste of each. Try Clapshaw at home once and you will never want to eat the two separately again.

If haggis is not to be the main course the choice to follow is often Roastit Beef or Roastit Bubblyjock (turkey) with all the trimmings. Turkey is a very popular choice today.

In times past dessert was usually such traditional dishes as Hattit Kit (a kind of curded milk) or Apple Frushie (apple tart), but nowadays anything goes, from Peach Melba to Coupe Jacques. Perhaps the most popular dessert is Sherry Trifle, served under a variety of names from Scotch Trifle to Tipsy Laird.

To round off the meal, bannocks or oatcakes follow, served with a kebbuck of cheese — preferably Dunlop Cheese from Ayrshire — or Crowdie ( a cream cheese). If your own area has a cheese ot its own, serve this by all means. Burns would approve of that! Although the evening is long it is a pity to rush such a meal, so it is always wise to start early and take time to enjoy the traditional dishes which are as much part of Burns Night as the speeches, recitations and songs.

The bill of fare can be set out in English or in Scottish dialect, something like this:

The Farin'

Cock-a-Leekie

Chieftain o' the Puddin' Race

Neeps and Nips

Roastit Stirk

wi' a' the trimmin's

Tipsy Laird

Kebbuck an' Oatcakes

Coffee

## THE PRINTER'S BILL

Invitations to the Burns Supper, the bill of fare and the toast lists are usually printed, unless the celebration is to be an informal one at which costs have to be kept to a minimum. Nowadays, with electric typewriters and marvellous duplicating facilities easily available, printed matter can be produced cheaply and easily but perhaps lacking the professional look. Two points have to be borne in mind — the bill of fare on the table enhances the enjoyment of the evening and will be retained as a memento afterwards, and secondly it will still cost money to have it duplicated on good quality paper. So before you decide to "do it yourself", call on a couple of printers for estimates. You may be surprised how little more it costs to have them printed.

You can cut costs by avoiding the use of illustrations or tartan ribbons on the bill of fare or gilt edges on the invitation card. A simple white card, well printed in blue to suggest the colours of the Saltire, will give a Scottish effect, look really good and give status to the occasion.

Always obtain estimates from at least two printers and ask in advance if printing 75 menu cards is the kind of work they specialise in. It is no good going to a firm which is geared to supplying half a million leaflets to a Government Department and expecting it to compete with a small man who does bills and invitations for local societies all the year round.

Ask secretaries of other societies to recommend names of printers, then go along and discuss your print requirements and ask for estimates in writing.

### THE SPEECHES

With venues and meal arranged, it is now time to think about the programme of speeches and entertainment which will follow. Two toasts, the Immortal Memory and the toast to the Lassies, are obligatory: others are optional at the discretion of the organisers, and can be to the Club or Society running the function, to the town or district, to Scotland, or (in the case of dinners overseas) the host country. Usually an appreciation of the Immortal Memory is also given.

### COSTING IT OUT

These speeches and the entertainment are dealt with fully in Chapters 8 and 9, so all that need be said here is that speakers, singers and musicians should be booked in good time so any costs involved in fees to artistes or for travel should be worked out and added to the estimated cost of the meal, entertainment of guests, printing of bill of fare and invitation cards, postage and other anticipated expenses. Remember to include VAT or service charge and add on a small margin for unexpected extras. Divide this total by the number of tickets you expect to sell and you have the price which must be charged for tickets. Remember the margin between profit and loss is a narrow one; it is also the margin between worry and peace of mind for the organiser, so check all the costs carefully before settling on a ticket selling price and err on the side of caution, so that you will not be faced with a loss.

## CHECK IN JANUARY

At the beginning of January every detail should be checked with the hotel manager again, and speakers and artistes reminded of their commitments. It may sound foolish to suggest that the man who is to propose the Immortal Memory may forget or have double booked, but it can happen easily. Popular speakers are trysted years ahead — often over the table at some other dinner or in the street — and it is easy for them to forget to put it into their diary later. By all means seize the chance to book someone when you meet him in the street, but follow the invitation up by letter at once, keeping a copy for your file.

That way, nothing will be left to chance on The Night.

## THE NIGHT

Time has flown since that day, probably the

best part of a year ago when the first inspection was made of the venue and it was decided to hold your Burns Supper there. Tickets have sold well, principal guests have all confirmed that they will be present, and programmes have arrived from the printers, been checked and found to be perfect. That's a relief!

The last few days have brought telephone calls to notify cancellations due to illness or other reasons, and these places have been taken up quickly by late-comers who have heard on the Burnsian grapevine that this promises to be one of the best Dinners of the year. Other callers ask for special places in the room to be beside friends or near the top table for someone who is a bit hard of hearing.

However trivial or unimportant each request may sound in relation to the enormous task of organising the evening, it is important to the person who is making it and has to be dealt with sympathetically and efficiently. People feel strongly about Burns, and they feel equally strongly about Burns Suppers; many a storm has blown up, and many a friendship has foundered because of a demand for special treatment at a Burns Supper which could not be met. Solomon and Job together could not produce a solution acceptable to some people, and it is foolish to try — better be firm at the start and say the request cannot be met than build up hopes only to dash them later.

## THE SEATING PLAN

One way or another the seating plan will give a headache for days, and may well not be settled satisfactorily until every member of the company is seated. Some clubs never allocate places, but let it be first come first served. In these cases guests arrive an hour or more before the Dinner and when the doors are opened make an undignified scramble for places near the speakers. Even then there are complaints of places being taken unfairly, or even of scarves and bags placed on chairs to reserve places, being switched.

My own preference is for a table plan to be prepared in advance with seats allocated so that guests and committee members are interspersed among the other members. The musicians and singers should be at tables seated near the piano so that they can be in position quickly when called upon to perform.

Whatever method is adopted, the organiser needs an efficient band of helpers to cope with seating problems at the start of the function. He will have plenty of other things on his mind at that time without having to worry about the fact that Mr.MacGregor's hearing-aid battery is flat so he needs a place under the nose of the principal speaker.

This is a long day for the organiser; final adjustments will have to be made to the seating plan and the actual plan typed out to be pinned on a board in the room where the reception is being held. A second plan for the VIP reception is a sound idea; that way the main guests will know what acquaintances are to be present. All morning the organiser will deal with queries, then he will want to visit the venue to make a last inspection and deliver the programmes, table-plans and other literature or display material needed. He will be back at the venue in good time to give his Chairman a final briefing, to allocate jobs to other officials and to be ready to receive the guests, looking as if he hadn't a care in the world.

## TOP TABLE PLAN

It will have been decided well in advance who sits at the top table. There are no hard and fast rules about numbers or placing, except that the principal speaker will be on the right of the Chairman, in the place of honour. Also at the Chaiman's table will be the other speakers, representatives of the Burns Federation, the clergyman who is to say grace, the local civic leader if present, and any other special guests the Chairman has chosen to invite. Husbands or wives of these guests will also be included in the top table party.

A special room is usually set aside for the Chairman and his guests, and they have their pre-dinner drinks there while the club members and their guests are gathering in the main room. When everybody is seated at table the top table party enter the dining room in procession, led by a piper. It is the organiser's job to arrange the procession in order as they are to sit at table starting with the person who is to be at the end on the left of the Chairman. At a signal the company stand and the Chairman and his guests enter and walk round the room clockwise to their places usually to handclaps from the waiting company. If the layout of the room is such that the top table party have to march in anticlockwise then the order will be reversed and start with the person who is to sit at the right-hand end of the table.

When the Chairman and principal guests have taken their places, the organiser can relax in theory at least. If he has done his preparatory work well and has a band of efficient helpers round him all should have gone smoothly so far.

HE CHAIRMAN takes charge of the proceedings the moment he reaches his place at table, and from then on success or failure becomes largely his responsibility. It is his duty to ensure that speeches, songs and music move along briskly but also with dignity and humour so that everyone goes home, as people ought to after a Burns Supper, feeling better folk.

Of course there must be fun at a Burns Supper — Burns would have insisted on it — but there must also be a serious element to it as well, especially in the Immortal Memory, which has not only to honour the Poet but must inspire the listeners to read Burns, to think about his achievement and as a result to improve their own lives. Burns is revered by Scots; he deserves respect, and the Immortal Memory must give him what is due to him.

The Chairman carries responsibility for this.

He also must put the whole company at ease from the start by showing that he himself is at ease. He should be neither indifferent nor diffident in his opening remarks, and a story, preferably with relevance to the club or group present is an excellent aid to this and, having put his stamp on the evening at this early stage, he must maintain the tone as he introduces each speaker or performer.

He carries the whole responsibility for the actual mechanics of the celebrations — when to serve each course of the meal and when to introduce each speaker or performer. He will ensure that he is seated within sight of the secretary so that he can give a signal if anything is not going according to plan or if some one needs a reminder to do his allotted task.

Serving staff have a job to do clearing courses and serving refreshments but not during the speeches and entertainment. Many Burns Suppers are ruined by waiters doing their work — they may think quietly — while speeches are being made or songs sung. The Chairman must see that this doesn't happen. At the same time he must give the serving staff an opportunity to do their job. A short pause between items allows for this, but the staff must be instructed to use this time.

The Chairman is usually the current year's President of the Club. If not he must be chosen with care and briefed in his duties and the aims of the Supper. If the President is in the chair, then he will have kept in close touch with the organiser all the year round, helping and advising on every aspect, but especially where the evening's speakers are concerned.

In many clubs the proposer of the Immortal Memory is the Chairman's guest — his personal choice of speaker — although he does usually consult the committee to make sure that he has secured the very best talent available. In other clubs the whole committee pools its knowledge of speakers and takes a vote to decide which shall be chosen. The secretary will write to invite him to speak, but the Chairman (probably accompanied by one or two committee members) will brief him nearer the time of the dinner on what the club expects of him and what the "tone" of the evening will be.

Burns Suppers come in many degrees of what *Punch* at the Festival of 1844 called "earnestness", and the Chairman will see that on The Night the right degree of earnestness is maintained.

Because he is President of the Club the Chairman will be a long-standing and respected member, well aware of the club's aims and aspirations. He may have served as Vice-President and, in that office, will have helped and advised the previous Chairman. The vice-presidency can be regarded as a rehearsal for this evening, this crowning event of his year of office as President.

During his vice-presidency the Chairman will have learnt much that will give him confidence tonight, but he will be nervous just like all the other "performers".

The Chairman must be serious most of the time, but not solemn. A joke or two will thaw the company, but that does not mean he should try to be a fast-talking comedian. There is nothing more painful to an audience than listening to an unfunny person trying to be funny. Every man knows in his own heart where he stands as a teller of funny stories, so it is up to him to tailor what he says to his own personality. Do not rely on others to tell you whether your jokes have gone down well or not — you can sense the reaction of the audience and get a more honest answer from inside your own head.

Notes. Do you need them? Again, only you know whether you are likely to forget vital points or even to dry up if you don't have something in writing to remind you. For me notes are the key to getting everything right on The Night; but they should not be so full that they can be read off the paper. Only a competent actor could deliver such a script convincingly. A few key points are really all that is needed as an *aide memoire.*

Quotations are a different matter. The most practised of speakers can dry up in the middle of a poem to the intense embarrassment of himself and his audience. It is a good idea to have quotations written out on a small piece of paper so that they can be consulted unobtrusively if necessary. Be certain that any quotations you intend to use are not a vital part of what a guest speaker has to say — you could so easily ruin his speech by using his key quotation first. So tell the speaker which quotations you intend to use.

It is always useful to have a full programme in front of you, giving names of songs, poems and performers, although these are printed on the bill of fare and programme of events for the evening. If they have not been printed, type them out on a sheet of paper and let this lie on the table so that you can work down the list item by item, without fear of omitting anything or anyone.

Check carefully the background of every speaker or performer so that he can be introduced in a proper way and no relevant detail forgotten. If he has written a book on Burns, mention it, if he is noted locally as a pigeon-fancier, refer to that. It is only courteous to give his background, especially highlighting a point which links him with Burns. If that seems too obvious a point, let me merely say that I have been introduced by Chairmen who have gone into all the detail about my early life and career and omitted to say that I have written books on Burns.

Getting details of the background of your speakers or performers wrong is as bad as getting their names wrong. It is important to them that they should be correctly presented to the gathering, so the Chairman should be courteous enough to ensure that his introduction is correct and brings out aspects of their background which are not only relevant but the ones they would like presented.

The Chairman's first job is to welcome the company, which should be done in a few short, friendly sentences. There is no need to go into detail about the speakers at this stage — merely to extend a welcome to them, to other important guests and to the assembled company generally, wishing them all a happy evening of companionship through Robert Burns, who himself liked nothing better than to be among friends, enjoying good food, a dram, and companionship.

Grace follows, and if the club has an honorary padre or another clergyman present, then it can be delegated to him: otherwise the Chairman will say grace.

The usual and most appropriate grace is the *Selkirk Grace*, which is regarded as the Poet's own special one, although it has little connection with him or with the Border town of Selkirk.

*The Selkirk Grace* was first attributed to Burns by Allan Cunningham in his 1834 edition of Burns. I have seen this grace referred to as *The Covenanter's Grace,* putting it a century before Burns, but Cunningham lifted it from a Belfast newspaper and palmed it off on to Burns — as he did with so many other things! Burns was supposed to have said the grace while visiting the Earl of Selkirk's home at St. Mary's Isle in Kirkcudbright, hence the name. Burns probably did use it, but he did not write it. The correct version of the *Selkirk Grace* is-

Some have meat and cannot eat,
    Some can not eat that want it:
But we have meat and we can eat
    Sae let the Lord be thankit.

It is more common to render the Grace in its earlier wholly-Scottish version, and in the light of its tenuous Burns connection this is fair enough:

Some hae meat and canna eat,
    And some wad eat that want it:
But we hae meat and we can eat
    And sae the Lord be thankit.

The first course of the dinner is now served, enjoyed and cleared, and the Chairman rises to welcome the haggis.

# ENTER THE HAGGIS

HE HAGGIS forms the central part of the bill of fare and, Immortal Memory apart, the focus of the evening because this is a dish which takes every Scot back to the way of life in Burns's time. Alongside oatmeal, it links our generation and that of our forefathers who made Scotland what she is today.

The haggis is a lordly dish of excellent pedigree, but it is a myth to say that it was given to us by the French and derives its name from the French word *hachis*, meaning minced meat. If the haggis was a culinary gift of the Auld Alliance between France and Scotland it is much more likely that it was the Scots who gave it to the French rather than the other way round.

F. Marian McNeill, in her classic work, *The Scots Kitchen*, points out that the name haggis is more likely to be derived from the old Scottish word to hag which means to hack or to chop. This is how Mrs. McNeill describes it. "The haggis is in fact simply a superior sausage, or, as Burns describes it, the 'great chieftain o' the puddin (sausage) race' ", and like the sausage it was once common to many lands. Of course the contents must have varied as much as do those of the sausage in our own time. To such as still 'look down wi' sneerin', scornfu' view on sic a dinner', we would point out that the most aesthetic of nations, the ancient Greeks, had a haggis of their own, which was immortalised by Aristophanes in *The Clouds*".

The haggis as Burns knew it and as we know it today is a tribute to the Scottish gift of making something of excellence out of cheap materials. Its ingredients are heart, lights and liver, beef-suet, oatmeal and onions minced together and sewn into the large stomach bag of a sheep.

The perfect haggis is neither so dry that it crumbles like cake, nor so wet that it clings to fork and plate and then to the palate. Haggis makers who can get the blend right spend busy weeks in January to satisfy the demand which comes to them from every quarter.

Alas, haggis is almost never made at home nowadays even in Scotland, which is a pity for one of the most memorable things I ever ate as a child was a haggis which my mother made according to an old recipe. As I remember it, mother's haggis was rather like a mealy pudding, but not over spicy, and had a slight sweetness to it. It was enormous and seemed to last for days, eaten first in the traditional way with potatoes and turnip (swede to the English), and then sliced cold and fried or toasted in front of the old kitchen range.

It was an experience to eat; a memory to be treasured. Never since have I tasted haggis like it, and the great pity is that I remember her making it only once.

F. Marian McNeill gives a recipe for a traditional haggis, and this is it. The ingredients are — the large stomach bag of a sheep, the pluck (including heart, lights and liver), beef-suet, pinhead (coarse) oatmeal, onions, black pepper, salt, stock or gravy.

This is her method:
"Brown and birstle (dry or toast) a breakfast cupful of oatmeal before the fire or in the oven. Clean the great bag thoroughly, washing it first in cold water and then, after turning it inside out, scalding and scraping it with a knife; then let it soak overnight in cold salted water. In the morning put it aside with the rough side turned out. Wash the pluck well and put on to boil covered with cold water, letting the windpipe hang over the side of the pot to let out any any impurities. Let it boil for a hour and a half, then take it out and cut away the pipes and any superfluities of gristle. Mince the heart and lights and grate half the liver. (The rest of the liver is not required). Put the minced and grated meat into a basin with half a pound of minced suet, two medium-sized onions finely chopped, and the toasted oatmeal, and season highly with black pepper and salt. (A pinch of cayenne say some housewives, 'makes all the difference'). Over the whole pour, preferably when cold, as much of the liquid in which the pluck was boiled (or better still, good stock) as will make the mixture sappy. Fill the stomach bag rather more than half full — say five-eighths — as it requires plenty of room to

swell. Sew it up securely and place it on an enamel plate in a pot of boiling water (to which half a pint of milk is often added), or, better still, boil it in stock. As soon as it begins to swell, prick it all over with a large needle to prevent its bursting. Boil steadily, without the lid, for three hours, adding boiling water as required to keep the haggis covered. Serve very hot without any garnish".

The usual accompaniments are mashed potatoes and mashed turnip or, better still, the two mashed together with pepper and a good piece of dripping as the delicious Orkney dish called Clapshaw. A little lean mutton may be substituted for the lights.

Should the haggis be made some time before it is wanted, re-heat by putting it into a pot of boiling water and letting it simmer (uncovered, for an hour or longer, according to size).

To enjoy haggis to the full it should be eaten slowly and savoured afterwards. This is why I like to see it occasionally as the main course of the evening, rather than a mere entertainment between two other courses. Even if the haggis is not the main course its presentation, service and enjoyment should not be skimped — Give the company long enough to admire it, to think about it, to savour it, and to reflect on what they have lost by letting it disappear from the daily menu.

Everybody enjoys the ritual presentation of the haggis and the address to it at table on Burns Night, and this seldom varies.

When the preceding course has been cleared and the signal comes from the kitchen that the haggis is ready, the Chairman calls on the company to stand to receive the haggis. The "beastie" is carried in by the chef or his representative, preceded by a piper who plays as the little procession marches round the room, usually to a slow handclap from the company, follwed by a third person carrying two bottles of whisky from which chef and piper are offered a dram later. In fact, a prudent Chairman arranges for two glasses of whisky to be placed on the table in advance, ready to be offered to the chef and piper. I have heard of the haggis being fiddled in instead of piped, and I have a sneaking feeling that Burns, who loved fiddle music, would have enjoyed that, but more usually it is a piper who does the honours in leading the dish to the table.

The bagpiper is one person whose invitation to play at the supper can be easily overlooked, and at Chesterfield, in Derbyshire, I'm told the Burns Club solved the problem neatly by making the piper an honorary life member!

When the haggis has been placed on the table a glass of whisky is offered to the chef and the piper who will drink it usually with a traditional Gaelic toast of "Slainte mhath" (your good health). The piper and chef leave and the *To a Haggis* is recited either by the Chairman himself or another person who has been delegated to do the honours. The poem may be read but it sounds far, far better recited from memory. A knife, the most forgotten item at a Burns Supper, should lie on the table so that, at the line "An' cut you up wi' ready slight" the haggis can be cut open. It is better for the people to be seated during the recitation of *To a*

*Haggis* to allow them to have a better view of the ceremony of cutting the haggis open.

How the haggis, innocent creature that it is, can be ill treated at this moment! After being welcomed like the returning prodigal it is sometimes fallen upon with such venom that the knife shoots clean through the silver flat on which it rests, and pins both to the table. If the plate is a china one, then it smashes into smithereens, and I have heard of at least one occasion when this resulted in a fierce altercation to decide who should pay for the plate! Others attack the haggis wildly and with eyes closed tightly, all but sever the hand that holds the plate.

At the other end of the scale there are the diffident haggis addressers who slide the knife along the bag so gently that the dirk glances off and the haggis slips to the floor.

Cutting the haggis bag open looks easy, but it is an art which comes only with practice. Remember the object of opening the bag is to reach the meat inside, and not to stab the haggis to death or to produce an incision to make some exploratory surgical operation, so a good plan is to make two incisions in the form of a St. Andrews Cross so that the bag can be folded back and the inside spooned out.

When the Address to the haggis is finished the company applauses or stands again to toast the haggis. If whisky is not being served to all guests, those members of the company who like whisky with their haggis will have ordered their dram in time to join in the toast. There is no need to down the whisky at a draught; after the toast they can sit down and savour it slowly with the haggis, bashed neeps and champit tatties. I have often seen the whisky poured over the haggis — a custom I have never been able to bring myself to adopt! It does nothing for haggis and it spoils the taste of excellent whisky.

## TO A HAGGIS

Fair fa' your honest, sonsie* face,     * plump
Great Chieftain o' the Puddin-race!
Aboon them a' ye tak your place,
    Painch, tripe or thairm: *     * intestine
Weel are ye wordy of a grace
    As lang's my arm.

The groaning trencher there ye fill,
Your hurdies* like a distant hill,     * buttocks
Your pin wad help to mend a mill
    In time o' need,
While thro' your pores the dews distil
    Like amber bead.

His knife see Rustic-labour dight, *     * wipe
An' cut you up wi' ready slight,
Trenching your gushing entrails bright
    Like onie ditch;
And then, O what a glorious sight,
    Warm-reekin, rich!

Then, horn for horn they stretch an' strive,
Deil tak the hindmost, on they drive,
Till a' their weel-swall'd kytes belyve*     * quickly
    Are bent like drums;
Then auld Guidman, maist like to rise,
    'Bethankit!' hums.

Is there that owre his French ragout,
Or olio wad staw* a sow,     * sicken
Or fricassee wad mak her spew
    Wi' perfect scunner,*     * revulsion

Looks down wi' sneering, scornfu' view
        On sic a dinner?

Poor devil! see him owre his trash,
As feckless as a wither'd rash,
His spindle shank a guid whip-lash
        His nieve* a nit*                          * fist  * nut
Thro' bluidy flood or field to dash,
        O how unfit!

But mark the Rustic, haggis-fed,
The trembling earth resounds his tread,
Clap in his walie* nieve a blade,                  * large
        He'll mak it whissle;
An' legs, an' arms, an' heads will sned,*      * be cut off
        Like taps o' thrissle.*                    * thistle

Ye pow'rs wha mak mankind your care,
And dish them out their bill o' fare,
Auld Scotland wants nae skinking* ware,        * watery
        That jaups in luggies;*               * milk-pails
But, if ye wish her gratefu' pray'r,
        Gie her a Haggis!

ith relief the Chairman can now settle down to enjoy his haggis, roastit bubbly-jock and crowdie cheese without a care until the last plate has been cleared.

Just as at any other function there will be many who will want to smoke as soon as the meal is over, and they will be waiting patiently for the Chairman to propose the Loyal Toast and grant permission to smoke as the coffee is being served.

Coffee and the interval before the speeches form an interlude during which guests, officials and members of the company can relax before the serious business of paying tribute to the Bard begins. This is an opportune moment for messages of good wishes from other societies to be read, or for formal Club business announcements to be made. Tickets for other functions run by the Club can be sold and raffle tickets for Burns or other charities can be taken round.

The Burns Federation certainly would be grateful at this time for a mention of its good work, and for copies of the annual *Burns Chronicle* to be sold. The *Chronicle* is certainly an excellent introduction to Burns for anyone who is unfamiliar with the Poet or his writings. It contains articles reflecting deep research into lesser known aspects of his life and work and gives the non-Burnsian some indication of the dimension of good which the Federation is doing for Scottish literature and the Scots way of life generally. Certainly the *Chronicle* contains enough thought-provoking material to fan the smallest spark of interest in Burns into a great fire of enthusiasm for the man and his achievement.

The Federation would also approve of a collection in aid of a Burns-linked charity such as the National Burns Memorial and Cottage Homes, or the Jean Armour Burns Houses at Mauchline. Alternatively, a collection might be made towards some broadly-based cultural charity like the Scottish National Dictionary to which the Federation has contributed much time and effort over many years.

The Scottish National Dictionary Association has already completed publication of a 10-volume record of the Scottish language, spoken and written, since 1700, and now it is working on a seven-year project to publish a definitive single-volume dictionary of Scots. Monies collected should be sent to The Secretary, Scottish National Dictionary, 27 George Square, Edinburgh, EH8 9LD.

The National Burns Memorial and Cottage Homes were established in 1896 to mark the centenary of the Poet's death, and comprise 20 houses for the elderly, clustered round a tall turreted tower on the land of Mossgiel farm at Mauchline, where Robert Burns worked so hard to hold his family together after his father's death. These cottages surely are just the kind of memorial of which the Poet would have approved — far more to his liking than statues or marble mausoleums. Information about the Memorial Homes and their financial needs can be obtained from The Secretary and Treasurer, The National Burns Memorial and Cottage Homes, 53 Bothwell Street, Glasgow, G2 6TE.

Although the Lassies are always remembered on Burns Night and there are memorials to Highland Mary Campbell, the Poet's wife, Jean Armour, was long neglected until Glasgow and District Burns Association built a group of 10 houses at Mauchline to mark the bicentenary of Burns's birth in 1959. Like the Cottage Homes these Jean Armour Burns Houses were also built on Mossgiel farmland, and they serve a very real need by providing homes for women who are self-sufficient but lack suitable living accommodation. The Association needs funds to maintain these 10 original houses and add to their number. Information can be obtained from Scott I. Galt, Hon. Secretary and Treasurer, Jean Armour Burns Houses, 8 Buchanan Street, Glasgow, G1 3LL.

When Coffee is finished, announcements made and collections have been completed the Chairman can announce an intermission — 10 minutes to 15 minutes — before the speeches and entertainment begin.

If the programme is to be a long one — and some Burns celebrations can last until two in the morning — then a second interval will follow half way through the entertainment.

## IMMORTAL MEMORY

**T**he company has reassembled, chairs are set back, glasses are filled, and it is time to get down to the serious business of honouring the memory of Robert Burns. This does not mean two solemn hours — or even two dull hours — of sombre eulogy after which nobody wants to hear the Bard's name mentioned for another twelvemonth at least.

My own views on this part of the Burns Night celebration are mixed. Worship of the Poet to the exclusion of every Scottish writer before or since his time, seems to contradict what the Poet worked for — he was a man who was inspired by writers who had preceded him in both Scotland and England. He took an interest even in French thought and Latin literature. Burns was never a nationalist in the narrow meaning of the word — his life stretched far beyond Scotland although he hardly ever crossed the Border. Yet to include the works of others can turn the evening into a kind of St. Andrews Night and obscure the real purpose of the January celebration — to honour Robert Burns. Certainly Burns himself admired the work of other poets and songwriters and enjoyed them as much as his own, and to that extent would be the first to want to share the celebration with them.

Perhaps the answer lies, where answers usually are to be found, somewhere in between. If appropriate, include a song or a poem by another writer, but make sure it is worthy of the evening. Otherwise stick to Burns — After all, if he is honoured in the right way, he will lead on to a greater interest in literature and even in the arts in general. Through Burns a wider audience can be brought to Scotland's great heritage of literature, from the early ballad-makers to present-day poets.

The mood for the Immortal Memory must be right and a couple of Burns songs or a selection of airs to his songs played on the fiddle will set the scene for the Chairman to call on his principal guest to propose the Immortal Memory of Robert Burns.


## PURPOSE OF THE IMMORTAL MEMORY

Before deciding who ought to propose the Immortal Memory it is as well to examine its purpose. It may go without saying that it is a toast to the memory of a great poet, but if it does that and no more, it will be an empty Immortal Memory.

What else should this key speech in the Burns Night celebration achieve?

A commentator, writing about the 1859 celebration marking the centenary of the Poet's birth — the first time the Burns movement stretched out to the world in an organised way — gave this reason for Burns's timeless appeal: "It is . . . partly because he represents his countrymen more thoroughly in their virtues and their failings then any other man of equal note among them". Few outside Scotland appreciate this, and for that reason they fail to understand properly why the Scots hold the Bard so dear. Burns helps Scots to take stock of themselves, of their way of life and of their fellow men, and the successful proposer of the Immortal Memory will interpret this for his listeners. In short, he will act as interpreter between the Poet and today's Scots.

The purpose of the Immortal Memory could be set out as fourfold:

To help people understand what Burns is saying;
To activate them to think about the reasons why Burns said what he did;
To encourage them to apply Burns's values to their own lives and to the social fabric around them, and resolve to improve both;
To persuade them to re-examine their country's nationhood, preserve it, and make it a force for good among their fellow nations.

If the speaker succeeds then he will have inspired his audience to try to rediscover their true selves, to think more kindly about their fellow men, and to want to make the world a better place.

## CHOICE OF SPEAKER

Finding a speaker who can command the respect of his listeners and inspire them is not easy. He has to be entertaining enough to hold his audience, yet must not be facile.

In the world of Burnsians a large number of people have made a reputation for themselves as good proposers of the Immortal Memory and are invited to travel the world to speak at Anniversary Dinners each year. They are in such demand that they must be booked more than a year in advance, and some even have full diaries for two or more years ahead.

If you can capture such a speaker well and good: if not, there is no need to despair — every community has its quota of good after-dinner speakers, and careful briefing can turn them into successful proposers of the Immortal Memory.

Club secretaries and committee members never stop the search for a speaker who will enhance their Dinner, and do better than those who make the speeches at rival club celebrations! Although there is plenty of cameraderie among Burns clubs and societies there is always rivalry to run the best Supper in the area. So club members attend other clubs' Dinners, listen critically and note names of speakers who ought to be invited to their Dinner another year. Burnsians talk among thenselves and an efficient secretary will have to be a good listener, a chiel amang his fellow Burnsians taking note of recommended speakers, especially "new faces" for Burns Night.

When a "new face" is found he is quickly asked to pencil into his diary a date a year or two years ahead, when he may be principal guest at the club's Dinner. A hurried consultation with other committee members then enables the secretary to write an official letter of invitation to confirm the provisional booking.

If no speaker comes to mind readily, then the Committee will meet very soon after one Annual Dinner to select a principal guest for next year. Debate in this meeting can be hot, and opinions expressed worthy of sharper Burns epigrams. Sometimes there is dissent over every name on the short list, but a vote has to be taken and a choice made.

In that way established Burns clubs find speakers. Those organising a Burns Supper for the first time or for a group other than a Burns society will not have the benefit of a committee's broad experience and will have to rely on their own ability to find the right person. Here the famous Burns "grapevine" will help.

By talking to people names of possible speakers will emerge, and with luck some of these will recur. These are the ones to consider seriously, although one must avoid the trap of choosing somebody who is an entertaining speaker but cares nothing for Burns.

If no suitable person can be found locally, then look further afield, discuss the problem with other Burns societies or with the Burns Federation in Kilmarnock. The Burns movement is a brotherhood, and will always help another organisation.

If the worst comes to the worst then you will have to fall back on a local personality with no reputation as a Burns speaker; choose a Scot if possible, a civic leader, a newspaper editor, a leading businessman — somebody with "go" to him, but don't assume that a man who can run the most prosperous factory in the district can make a good speech. Especially a speech about Robert Burns! Choose a person you have heard speak yourself if possible, and if you are in the way of attending dinners (Burns or others) listen critically whenever you go to a function, read local press reports, and listen to people being interviewed on the radio or television. In that way you can build up your own "bank" of speakers.

Having selected your possible speaker, arrange to meet him, talk to him about Burns, find out how much he is in sympathy with the Poet and his ideals. Explain to him the background of your own organisation, its objectives, and the reasons why it is holding a Burns Supper. In discussion you will be able to assess how willing your possible speaker is to be briefed and how well he is likely to perform on "The Night".

If you are satisfied that he measures up to your needs, ask him to put the date in his diary provisionally, then follow up with a confirmatory letter, giving full details — date, place and time of Dinner, length of time he will be expected to speak, names of other speakers if you know them, and suggest a date for a briefing meeting a month or six weeks in advance of the event.

What happens if your speaker is taken ill or is delayed by the notoriously bad weather which always seems to plague Burns Suppers? The answer is to be prepared to make the speech yourself or to warn a committee member that he may be called on — Of course if you have a few days notice you can usually find another Burnsian to make the speech. But never assume that you will not need a substitute until you actually see your principal guest walk into the room. Only then can you tell his understudy to relax.

## BRIEFING THE SPEAKER

Briefing should not be left to the Chairman alone: a small group of committee members should meet him informally to explain to him his part in the Night's proceedings. You have already explained something about your own association, but a reminder is no bad thing now, so take along as much printed literature about it as you can and leave it with him. Remind him of the type of Anniversary Dinner it is to be — formal or informal; a serious meeting of knowledgeable Burnsians or just folk with a passing interest in the Poet; a male gathering or mixed company; whether dress is formal or informal. Tell him how long you expect him to talk, who the other speakers are, what entertainment will follow, what guests are expected, and lastly remind him of the time of the Dinner and the people he can expect to meet. Put yourself in his place and ask what you would need to know to make the speech yourself and you will not go very far wrong.

On "The Night" your speaker will no doubt be nervous, so leave him as few surprises as you can. At one of the first Anniversary Dinners I ever addressed I discovered after I had sat down at the table that one of the guests was an important Burns Federation office-bearer. No one had thought to mention that he was to be present, or to introduce me to him during the pre-Dinner reception, and as a result I spent a miserable two hours until my speech was over, worrying about what this man who knew so much about Burns was going to think of my empty words. Only later, I discovered that he was a delightful man with a mind open enough to listen to a beginner like me!

## HOW LONG SHOULD IT BE

Most serious Burns Clubs ask for an Immortal Memory of 30 - 35 minutes and I have known a speaker to hold his audience spellbound for almost and hour. However, a far more acceptable length for the average speaker and average audience is 20 - 25 minutes.

## YOU HAVE BEEN ASKED TO SPEAK

This book is designed to help the person who has been asked to speak at a Burns Supper as much as for the person who is organising the event. Now it is time to throw the speaker a lifeline.

Before you begin to compile your speech let me offer a few general hints. Clear diction, a well modulated voice and a pace which allows the listeners to assimilate what is being said are all essential ingredients of any speech, whether it is about Robert Burns or life in Babylonian times. Again, it must be emphasised that length is vital: it must not be so long that it has to be gabbled to reach the end within reasonable time, so it must be practised thoroughly at home to get these mechanical points right.

Those who are fortunate enough to live within reach of the Burns Country would find inspiration by walking around the places connected with the Bard. Go to Alloway early in the day before other tourists arrive and stand beside the ingle to picture the family's daily life; stand by the Poet's father's grave in the Auld Kirk of Alloway and think about the relationship between father and son; feel the wind in your face on the high arch of the Brig O'Doon; and visit the Burns Centre to see the audio-visual interpretation of his life. There are other places to visit — Mount Oliphant, Leglen Wood, Lochlea, Mossgiel, Mauchline Kirk, and banks of Ayr, Doon and Nith, and of course Ellisland and the Poet's house at Dumfries. An hour's crack with Sam Hay, the delightful curator of the Bachelors' Club at Tarbolton, would be time well spent. Visit one or all of these places and use a little imagination to return to Burns's time and life-style. When you begin to read about the Poet, his life and achievement will suddenly come into focus.

When it comes to writing the speech, bear in mind Burns's own humility, and as a reminder set in front of you the words:

O wad some Power the giftie gie us
Tae see oursels as ithers see us!

With that in mind you will not go far astray.

## SUITABLE SUBJECTS

Like a sermon, a good Immortal Memory should start from a text, but there the kirk comparison should end. The speech should examine the theme and relate it to the listeners, quoting generously from Burns to underline the points being made. It should contain light and shadow but end with the Poet bathed in blazing light.

Burns Clubs expect their speakers to focus on an aspect of the Poet's life, and use it to demonstrate the great achievement of Robert Burns and the debt the world owes to him. Here is a selection of themes from Burns Suppers round the world taken at random from a single edition of the Burns Chronicle:

Burns — Ploughman or genius and intellectual;
Burns as a Man;
Exciseman and Farmer;
Folksong writer of genius;
Burns's thoughts if he were alive today;
Burns — Preserver of our heritage;
Farming in Ayrshire in Burns's time;
Dominies in Burns's day (speech by a schoolmaster);
Hame (at an exiles' Dinner)

Whatever the subject, the aim should be to relate it to the audience and to the Poet's work. The first step towards this is to read as widely as possible round the subject, taking in the views of Burns and others. Pay especial heed to what the Bard had to say and what comments others made on his views during his lifetime or after. Read the main biographies of the Poet by Hans Hecht, Catherine Carswell and Franklin Bliss Snyder, then follow these up with specialist books and articles on the subject you have chosen. Read the poems, both to set the mood for writing about Burns, and to find suiable quotations to illustrate the speech.

I suggest treatments for a few Immortal Memories to show how subjects might be tackled. The same principles can be applied to any other subject or theme to produce and Immortal Memory which will come over to the audience as fresh and interesting. These are not finished speeches but outlines round which a full

Immortal Memory can be built.

This is considered the easiest Immortal Memory, yet it is the hardest to hold the interest of the listener because it is covering well-trodden ground.

Rather than recite all the facts in chronological order you can give this speech a lift by choosing a theme and confining it to an aspect of the man. For example, you could take the words of Maria Riddell which at once admitted the imperfections of the Poet's life yet pointed to the genius — "It is only on the gem we are disturbed to see the dust. The pebble may be soiled, and we do not regard it."

Consider this statement against four periods of his life:

farm lad;
famous man;
man in love with mankind and womankind;
and sick man struggling to fulfil his destiny.

\* \* \*

*Farm lad:* Brother Gilbert suggests a rather lonely, inwardlooking boyhood when he says, "We rarely saw anybody but the members of our own family. There were no boys of our age, or near it, in the neighbourhood . . . My father was for some time almost the only companion we had." He also suggests that his brother tended to be jealous of others who were more fortunate than himself.

Yet Robert himself talks of meetings with young people in Ayr; of lessons with his teacher, John Murdoch; and, as he grew to young manhood, of the Bachelors' Club debating society which he helped to found in Tarbolton, the dancing classes which he attended, to his father's and the full social life with members of both sexes which he managed to maintain while working long and hard hours on the farm.

*The Cotter's Saturday Night* does not suggest an introverted young man or an introverted family:

> With joy unfeign'd, brothers and sisters meet,
>> And each for other's weelfare kindly spiers: * * asks
> The social hours, swift-wing'd, unnotic'd fleet;
>> Each tells the uncos* that he sees or hears.     * news
> The Parents partial eye their hopeful years;
>> Anticipation forward points the view;
> The mother wi' her needle and her sheers
>> Gars auld claes look amaist as weel's the new;
> The father mixes a' wi' admonition due.

Contrast this with satire against the Church and against injustice. Burns was in trouble with the Kirk because of his youthful love affairs; without these he would still have quarrelled with the Kirk or a section of it at least, because he could not bear the narrowness of strict Calvinism or hypocrisy. He satirized religion's least attractive features in *The Holy Fair*, one of a series of poems which caused a great furore throughout the countryside. He painted a picture in this poem so clear that folk could see themselves.

> Here some are thinkin on their sins,
>> An' some upo' their claes;

Ane  curses feet that fyl'd* his shins,                    * dirtied
        Anither sighs an' prays:
On this hand sits a chosen swatch,
        Wi' screw'd-up, grace-proud faces;
On that a set o' chaps, at watch,
        Thrang* winkin on the lasses                        * busy
                To chairs that day.

Small wonder the Kirk was alarmed. Then he
set upon one of its most hypocritical elders,
William Fisher, who had led an attack on Burns's
friend and landlord Gavin Hamilton. *Holy Willie's
Prayer* shows the young Burns at his sharp-
tongued best as he satirized the old elder who
knew he was among those chosen for salvation.
It's impossible to read the poem without hearing
Holy    Willie's    voice,    high-pitched    and
sanctimonious.

        Yet I am here, a chosen sample,
        To shew thy grace is great and ample:
        I'm here, a pillar o' thy temple
                Strong as a rock,
        A guide, a ruler and example
                To a' thy flock.

It's to Burns's credit that *Holy Willie's Prayer*
was written to defend his friend Gavin Hamilton,
rather than to attack Willie Fisher. *The Twa Dugs*
was an angry reaction to his father's lawsuit over
the farm lease at Lochlea, again pointing to the
poet's humanity in understanding the suffering of
the poor farmer.

        I've notic'd, on our Laird's court-day,
        An mony a time my heart's been wae,
        Poor tenant-bodies, scant o' cash,
        How they maun thole* a factor's snash;        * suffer
        He'll stamp an threaten, curse an swear,
        He'll apprehend them, poind their gear,

While they maun stand, wi' aspect humble,
An' hear it a', an fear an' tremble.

Already the gem was gleaming through.

*Famous man:* Fame came suddenly to Robert Burns. One day he was a farm lad fleeing the wrath of the kirk and of James Armour whose daughter he had made pregnant. Next he was author of a fast-selling book of poems, and was on his way to Edinburgh to negotiate a second. The pebble had indeed proved to be a gemstone, clearly reflecting its colours through the dust of the disgrace because of overfondness for the lassies and the sharp tongue with which he criticised the less attractive aspects of the Kirk.

In Edinburgh he presented the outward appearance of a ploughman, but many were not taken in and recognised his true genius. He himself was apprehensive about mixing with the great men of the capital, although he felt in no way inferior to them. Burns always knew where he stood. He wrote: "Never did Saul's armour sit so heavy on David when going to encounter Goliath, as does the encumbering robe of public notice with which the friendship and patronage of some 'names to fame' have invested me. — I do not say this in the ridiculous idea of seeming self-abasement, and affected modesty. — I have long studied myself, and I think I know pretty exactly what ground I occupy, both as a Man and a Poet . . . . "

We went through the motions of praising the city (Address to Edinburgh) yet must often have thought at this time of the words of his *Address to the Unco Guid* which applied to that smug society.

> O ye wha are sae guid yoursel,
>     Sae pious and sae holy,
> Ye've nought to do but mark and tell
>     Your neebours' faults and folly!

Sometimes his pen wounded others deeply, but those were the very moments when he could turn about and make some simple and beautiful statement which showed true humanity, humility and understanding. In that same poem *The Unco Guid:*

> Then gently scan your brother Man,
>     Still gentler sister Woman;
> Tho' they may gang a kennin* wrang,     * little
>     To step aside is human:
> One point must still be greatly dark,
>     The moving *why* they do it;
> And just as lamely can ye mark,
>     How far perhaps they rue it.
>
> Who made the heart, 'tis He alone
>     Decidedly can try us,
> He knows each chord, its various tone,
>     Each spring its various bias:
> Then at the balance let's be mute,
>     We never can adjust it;
> What's done we partly may compute,
>     But know not what's resisted.

The dust of sharp criticism is at once swept away by perfect understanding.

*The man in love:* Burns has plenty of critics here who can be quoted, from his own family's despair at the all-too-apparent results of his love-making to the strictures of his first biographer, Dr. James Currie. And the Poet himself can be quoted in support of or against his weakness for womankind. Yet there is ample evidence that women sought out Burns as much as he ever sought them.

Burns's love ran to more than broken hearts and illegitimate children. From it flowed songs and poems describing every aspect of the emotion from a young girl's plea that she's owre young to marry yet to the companionship of old age in *John Anderson My Jo.*

> John Anderson my jo, John,
>> We clamb the hill thegither;
> And mony a canty\* day, John,          \* happy
>> We've had wi' ane anither:
> Now we maun totter down, John,
>> And hand in hand we'll go;
> And sleep thegither at the foot,
>> John Anderson, my Jo.

*The sick man:* Here Burns needed all the compassion he had poured out to others and he was ill rewarded by his first biographer. Dr. Currie wrote that Burns's drinking affected his work, but this is nonsense. Burns was highly thought of by his Excise colleagues and when someone tried to denounce him to the powers in Edinburgh nothing was found against him. Burns's drinking was social — it was company he craved not whisky. Indeed his health would not have stood up to excessive drinking.

The glorious drunkenness of *Willie Brew'd a Peck o' Maut* is not the singing of the drunkard but the convivial carousal of the man who enjoys company and a dram, but just occasionally drifts over the edge of sobriety.

We are na fou,* we're nae that fou,                    * drunk
    But just a drappie in our e'e;
The cock may craw, the day may daw,
    And ay we'll taste the barley bree.*        * whisky

\*   \*   \*

From each aspect of his life Burns created poetry which is a distillation of compassion, understanding and love for his fellow men. Even where his own life can be exposed to criticism he disarms his critics. The dust truly shows up the gem that lies underneath it.

In Burns's frailty can be found the basis of his immortality: where there appear to be depths, heights are suddenly discovered: where weakness shows through strength can be found.

Maria Riddell saw the true Burns, the man who inspires us still today, the man to whom we humbly offer our Immortal Memory.

## OUTLINE SPEECH 2
## PLOUGHMAN OR INTELLECTUAL

This Immortal Memory can take as its text the note Alison Chalmers sent to a friend after seeing Burns in Edinburgh. "The town is at present agog with the ploughman poet who receives adulation with native dignity, and is the very figure of his profession — strong and coarse — but has a most enthusiastick heart of LOVE".

The speech will contrast the farming background with Edinburgh society and show how Burns was remarkably well educated — educated beyond most of his equals. By his genius he was able to turn book learning into original thoughts and opinions which reached the core of man's being.

From early days he was a thinker, using his mind and forming his own point of view. He told how one of the first things he remenbered was seeing a pretty young maidservant in church being forced to rise to make way for the fat, pompous son of the local mansionhouse. And Burns carried that picture in his mind ever after. No doubt that was the seed of *A Man's a Man for A' That.*

> Ye see yon birkie* ca'd a lord,     * fine fellow
>     Wha struts, and stares, and a' that,
> Though hundreds worship at his word,
>     He's but a coof* for a' that.     * fool
> For a' that, and a' that,
>     His ribband, star and a' that,
> The man of independant mind,
>     He looks and laughs at a' that.

He showed early signs of intellectual agility in arguments with his friends, in his poems lambasting hypocrisy within the Church and of course in helping to establish the Bachelors' Club debating society in Tarbolton.

In Edinburgh he was Daniel in the lion's den. Yet he was not overawed by the great minds of that period which was known as Edinburgh's Golden Age. He was confident of his own ability because he had thought out where he stood and he knew that he deserved respect. Burns knew that he was as many miles ahead of thoses he met intellectually as his crude Ayrshire farming manners suggested that he was behind them socially. And, though people generally thought him an unlettered ploughman, there were plenty of great men in the capital who recognised his intellectual capacity.

Yet Burns was never at home among such society, and was drawn to the Crochallan Fencibles, a drinking club, rather than to the drawing rooms of the New Town. He was also pulled towards writing in the Doric instead of Augustan stanzas in standard English. Even his great and passionate love affair in Edinburgh, with Agnes Maclehose, was conducted on a high intellectual plane with Burns calling himself Sylvander and her Clarinda. Yet the affair produced a basic love song of deep human feeling, *Ae Fond Kiss.*

> I'll ne'er blame my partial fancy,
> Naething could resist my Nancy:
> But to see her, was to love her,
> Love but her, and love for ever.
>
> Had we never lov'd sae kindly,
> Hand we never lov'd sae blindly!
> Never met — or never parted,
> We had ne'er been broken-hearted.

Proof of the brilliance of Burns's intellect is found in the fact that people with brilliant minds sought him out for his company and his conversation — rich, influential, important people. Because Burns was the type of man that he was, Robert Graham of Fintry helped him to become an Exciseman and for the same reason Patrick Miller offered him the lease of Ellisland farm.

Burns's genius shines through his poetry, perhaps as brilliantly in *Tam O'Shanter* as in any other poem. Here he took a simple folk-tale and fashioned it into a great narrative poem, brilliantly constructed, written with genius. Examine the poem, in its various parts — the simplicity with which the scene is set in Ayr, the clarity with which Tam is described, the vividness of the hellish ongoings at Alloway's Auld Haunted Kirk.

Warlocks and witches in a dance;
Nae cotillion brent* new frae France,          * brand
But hornpipes, jigs, strathspeys, and reels,
Put life and mettle in their heels.
A winnock-bunker* in the east,          * window seat
There sat auld Nick, in shape o' beast;
A towzie tyke,* black, grim, and large,  * unkempt dog
To gie them music was his charge:
He screw'd the pipes and gart* them skirl,          * made
Till roof and rafters a' did dirl.*          * rattle

The search for the intellectual Robert Burns can be taken much further — to fit him in his niche among Scottish men of letters, to examine the elements of his work which are derived from earlier poets and literary sources.

His contemporaries were shrewd enough to recognise his genius, and to accept the "uneducated ploughman" as their intellectual superior, even if a few held back socially.

Burns allowed the ploughman myth to persist when he could easily have scotched it because it suited him to be thought a rustic genius by those who were not bright enough to recognise what he really was. Burns was a shrewd man who knew when to be the farmer and when to be the intellectual. And, oddly, he was at home in both roles.

Why should he not have been? For far too long the farm worker has been regarded as beneath his townsman peers, and it is only now that his true worth is being acknowledged. In Burns's time his work was endless and grinding and his reward miserly. Burns lifted him to a higher plane.

The truth is that Burns was both ploughman and intellectual, and it is as both that we salute him.


## OUTLINE SPEECH 3
### BURNS'S THOUGHTS IF HE WERE ALIVE TODAY

This is often considered a lighter Immortal Memory, but it need not be shallow.

There are enough injustices and inconsistencies in any community to provide material for the pen of a dozen Robert Burns. These can be exploited by a speaker who knows the community well.

Those who suffer delays of planning applications, slow builders and other impediments to getting jobs done, will find a chord of sympathy in Burns's worry when he was trying to hasten the building of his farmhouse at Ellisland so that he could be reunited with his wife, Jean, and their family:
"I am distressed with the want of my house in the most provoking manner" he wrote to the builder. "It loses me two hours' work of my servants every day, besides other inconveniences. For God's sake let me but within the shell of it". And the relief when he was finally settled in it with his wife Jean and able to sing:

O were I on Parnassus hill,
Or had o' Helicon my fill;
That I might catch poetic skill,
    To sing how dear I love thee.

Like the rest of us he could take umbrage easily and forgive equally easily. When the landlord at the inn in Inverary was too busy with the Duke of Argyll's guests to serve him he wrote:

There's naething here but Highland pride,
    And Highland scab and hunger,
If Providence has sent me here,
    'Twas surely in an anger.

Yet the same man could also write a touching little note of thanks:

When death's dark stream I ferry o'er,
    A time that surely shall come;
In Heaven itself, I'll ask no more,
    Than just a Highland welcome.

These apparently irreconcilable views are exactly like our own veering, inconsistent attitudes. Burns speaks as clearly as if he were with us still.

The theme can be broadened to examine national and international affairs and draw comparisons from the situation in Burns's time. There is quite enough hypocrisy and double dealing in the world to stimulate any man of independent mind just as there was in Scotland of the 1780s and 1790s. Injustice may not be quite so narrowly applied in our day when governments behave (in the name of the people) in the arrogant way in which individuals did in Burns's time but they exist and need to be exposed.

Were he alive today Burns would deplore the neglect of our native Scots tongue, and the abandonment of so many decent values. He would be horrified at the drift away from basic homegrown foods, and he would be sorry that his old, faithful friend, the horse, has been replaced by the motor-car and tractor. You can't chat or recite a poem to a combine harvester. He would deplore the kirk's decline, but he would point out the reasons and castigate those responsible. He would probably like television and radio, but would have plenty to say about their standards, perhaps even writing for them and thus improving them. And of course he would approve of such advances as preventive medicine, social justice and living standards.

However, it would be wrong to use the occasion merely to destroy that which is bad or to criticise wrongs. It should be a base for building up what is good, and here Burns relates to us clearly across two centuries — on patriotism, humanity, common decency and brotherly love.

Burns offers even more — pity and understanding. The mouse and the daisy spell out the fate of mankind, not merely the misfortune of a beast or flower in a field at Mossgiel. In how many places in the world at this exact moment could his pitying spirit stand beside a human family and say,

> Thy wee bit housie, too, in ruin!
> Its silly wa's the win's are strewin!
> An' naething, now, to big a new ane,
>     O' foggage green!
> An' bleak December's winds ensuin,
>     Baith snell* an' keen!          * cold

The cruelty of mankind is underlined by the animal's hopelessness but Burns quickly points out that for human beings the fear and misery have an added dimension because man is God's created, greater being:

> Still, thou art blest, compar'd wi' me!
> The present only toucheth thee:
> But Och! I backward cast my e'e
>     On prospects drear!
> An' forward, tho' I canna see,
>     I guess an' fear!

Through the years right down to today, Burns speaks clearly to us and points out our hopes and fears. If only mankind would listen to him and learn. Perhaps in drinking to Robert Burns's Immortal Memory we can make a start.

## OUTLINE SPEECH 4 — HAME

A favourite and appropriate subject for exiles, and one I have used in Scotland to remind Scots of what living outside Scotland means to those of us who are in "foreign parts", even if these are only across the Border in England.

There are many suitable texts in Burns's works from which to examine what home means to the Scot (e.g. the Jacobite songs like *The Highland Widow's Lament* which begins, "Oh, I am come to the low Countrie," or *It was a' for our Rightfu' King)* but why not start from someone else's view? Where better than the *Canadian Boating Song*, an anonymous poem which expresses longing for home as no other poem does?

From the lone shieling of the misty island
    Mountains divide us, and the waste of seas —
Yet still the blood is strong, the heart is Highland,
    And we in dreams behold the Hebrides.

This is a reminder both of what exile means and of the uneasy times in which Burns lived and it is easy to bridge two centuries to our own shifting times. Social change forced thousands to leave — unwilling emigrants — although one must not lose sight of the many adventurous Scots who through the centuries· have willingly gone overseas in search of fortune.

Burns himself nearly emigrated twice: to Jamaica to escape the wrath of Jean Armour's father, and to London where he was offered work as a journalist. That he stayed in Scotland was perhaps the most fortunate thing that happened for our country in all history, apart from Bannockburn.

Burns loved his homeland and he loved home. He recognised the importance of family life and its values and he summed these up in *"The Cotter's Saturday Night"*, the poem which means family life to the Scot:

Belyve, the elder bairns come drapping in,
    At service out, among the farmers roun';
Some ca' the pleugh, some herd, some tentie* rin  * carefully
    A cannie errand to a neebor town:
Their eldest hope, their Jenny, woman-grown,
    In youthfu' bloom, love sparkling in her e'e,
Comes hame, perhaps to show a braw new gown,
    Or deposite her sair-won penny-fee,
To help her parents dear, if they in hardship be.

Burns loved Scotland too, and concerned himself with all aspects of life there — political, religious and social. He spelt out clearly where he thought it failed the people, a brave thing to do in the 18th Century when autocratic governments had powers to silence their critics. Are there not parallels today?

Burns's greatest gift to the exile, however, was to preserve his heritage and give it a timelessness which extends across the globe and even across generations of time. Two main ingredients of this are his songs and language.

*Songs:* Burns revived the all-but-lost tradition of folk song. He wrote over 300 songs, many of them new versions of older ones, many of them new words to traditional tunes going back even beyond the Reformation. Here he was exposing something which lay below the surface of consciousness, and naturally Scottish hearts responded.

*Language:* Like all creative young men, Burns experimented before settling on a way of expressing himself which suited him best. He tried standard English but rejected it for the vernacular, and we should be thankful he did. Language is a key ingredient in the preservation of any people's nationhood.

Decent values, the Scots tongue and Burns's heritage of song were almost all that many Scots had to take with them when they sailed to make new lives in other parts of the world. They were enough to make home a magnet to which their thoughts were drawn even after several generations, by which time they were completely integrated into their new homelands.

# THE OTHER SPEECHES

NLY TWO other speeches are obligatory — the Toast to the Lassies and the Response to that toast. An Appreciation of the Immortal Memory is usually given also, and this is a courtesy which the principal speaker appreciates. I have been to dinners where, instead of an appreciation of the Immortal Memory, the speaker has been invited later on in the evening to say a few words of appreciation of the club.

The length of these speeches will depend on the rest of the programme, the formality of the whole celebration, and perhaps on which other organisations are present and have to be recognised. Regardless of all these factors, speeches should never extend beyond 10 minutes, and less is desirable. Six to seven minutes is ideal, with the reply slightly shorter.

But how do you stop a speaker when he is in full flow? You don't; you suffer. It is easier to stop him before he begins, if that doesn't sound too Irish. When you invite him, make it clear that he will have six minutes and must not talk beyond that allotted time. Refer to this limit in his letter of invitation, remind him again when he is briefed a month or so before the dinner, and give him a detailed programme for the evening, including timings. On the night itself give another firm, friendly reminder. If anyone overruns his time after that, never never invite him again, and don't recommend him to anyone else.

When you are asking other Clubs about possible speakers always find out whether they are men who habitually overrun their time, and in return when you are asked to advise on speakers, make it clear whether they can be trusted to abide by the programme timing. There is nothing worse for guests and organiser alike than to find the programme over-running by half an hour or more, so that some of the entertainment has to be dropped, which is not fair to the audience or artistes — a long-winded bore is no substitute for a couple of Burns songs.

The Immortal Memory is the serious work of the evening : the other speeches, apart from the Appreciation, are the fun. They should therefore be lighthearted and humorous, and aim to entertain every bit as much as the songs and recitations among which they are interspersed.

## THE APPRECIATION

This is usually given by a member of the company with a deep knowledge of Burns, who will speak briefly (say five minutes) on the topic which the proposer has chosen, reminding the company of salient points and of the relevance of the Bard to their lives, as referred to in the speech. He will thank the proposer and naturally, if the job has been done well, give fulsome praise. The Appreciation is brief, but it is important because it lends extra authority to what has been said in the Immortal Memory.

## THE LASSIES

If there is a joker in the pack, play him now! The Toast to the Lassies should be the most amusing speech of the evening.

I notice that some programmes say "Lassies" and others "Lasses". Which is correct? Both in fact, and the only explanation of the difference which I can offer is the "Lasses" is the plural of the word "lass" which is a standard English word. "Lassie", on the other hand, is purely Scottish. For that reason I prefer the programme to say, "The Lassies".

If you cannot make up your mind which you prefer you can entitle the toast "Bonnie Jean" and associate it with the Poet's wife and wifely virtue in general.

The toast varies according to whether the Dinner is all-male or mixed company. If there are women present then it is a speech teasing womenfolk for their shortcoming as pointed out by Burns. There are plenty of examples from which to choose — from Tam O' Shanter's wife to the strong-minded landlady with whom the Poet lodged on his first visit to Edinburgh ; from Maria Riddell's teasing of his emotions to Willie Wastle's harridan at Linkumdoddie.

Willie Wastle dwells on Tweed,
    The spot they ca' it Linkumdoddie,
A creeshie* webster till his trade,      * greasy/filthy
    Can steal a clue wi' any body;
He has a wife that's dour and din,
    Tinkler Madgie was her mither,
Sic a wife as Willie's wife,
    I wadna gie a button for her.

This should be a racy speech, with plenty of jokes and fun poked at womankind in our society. There's a lot of scope in these days of "Women's Lib" and laws which forbid one from advertising for a charwoman or even a chairwoman.

Gentle fun is the key to this speech, and it must always end on a complimentary note, again referring to Burns, his patient, understanding wife, and his basic respect for the female sex.

At the end of his speech the proposer will ask the men to rise and join him in drinking the toast to the Lassies.

## THE RESPONSE

The Toast to the Lassies is a battle of the sexes, and in the response, women have a chance to get their revenge. Now they can take men to task for their shortcomings, especially their chauvinism, drinking and abuse of woman's love for them. Burns can be used to back this up too, especially to make the point that, without the lassies, man seldom amounts to very much in life.

No matter what may have been said about the lassies, Burns gives them the unanswerable retort to the menfolk. In *Green Grow the Rashes O* he writes:

> Auld Nature swears, the lovely Dears
> Her noblest work she classes, O:
> Her prentice han' she try'd on man,
> An' then she made the lasses, O.

Behind most successful men there is a woman which was true of Burns, who had Jean Armour. Take away the lassies and what would be left of Burns's songs? But again the speech should end by complimenting the opposite sex.

In cold print the Toast to the Lassies may sound an outdated, chauvinist display, out of tune with modern life. In practice it is a highly enjoyable part of the evening, which still goes down well.

## OTHER TOASTS

The number of other speeches will depend on the nature of the occasion and who is present. If a civic leader is attending, then obviously it would be respectful to toast his town or area and it would flatter him to be given the chance to speak. On the programme this goes under many titles, "Our Town", "The City of ....", "Oor Toon", and so on. At Dinners where the majority of those attending are exiled Scots, the toast becomes "The Town of our Adoption", or even "The Land of our Adoption".

This toast can be combined with the general toast to the guests if the number of speeches is limited.

Scotland features as a toast on many Burns Night programmes, and rightly so. Titles vary to suit taste — "Scotland", or "Scotia", "Auld Scotland", "Auld Scotia", (or even "Puir Auld Scotland"). Overseas, this toast becomes "The Land we Left". At exiles' Dinners it is right to honour the country in which the celebration is taking place, so a toast to "Land of our Adoption" is appropriate, or one coupling that country with Scotland, under the title "Two Lands".

The Burns movement is included in the toast list of many organisations — "The Burns

Federation" or "Kindred Clubs". And if a prominent Federation representative is present this will give him the chance to talk about the aims and achievements of the Federation and of the Burns movement generally.

# SANGS AND CLATTER

**R**EMEMBER HOW in Tam O'Shanter the "night drave on wi' sangs and clatter; And ay the ale was growing better"? That is how Burns Night should go, with plenty of songs and music and recitations. No particular works of Burns have to be included, but clubs have their own favourites which are always on their programme.

*Tam O'Shanter* is probably the most popular poem for Burns Night recitation, *with Holy Willie's Prayer* and the *Address to the Unco Guid* as alternatives. *The Cotter's Saturday Night* is another recitation which goes down well, but of course it is always good to surprise the company with something "different", like *Death and Dr. Hornbook* or perhaps *The Two Dugs* recited by two people.

If you have a really good performer available try a longer poem by all means, but if you are uncertain about the quality of your verse speaker then select two shorter poems rather than one long one, and space them well apart in the programme.

As there are usually a number of non-Burnsians present at any Dinner, it is a good idea when introducing the poem to say a few words about its origin and to explain what it is about.

Songs and Burns can never be separated. He wrote more than three hundred of them, practically every one a gem, and ranging from love and drinking songs to patriotic and political ones. No wonder the Burns Night celebrations ends with someone regretting that a particular favourite has been missed out.

The only advice to be given on choosing appropriate songs for a Burns Night programme is that they should cover a wide range of Burns's themes to display his genius. Otherwise, be guided by whatever your singers feel they can sing best, or if you are anxious to include a certain song, then find a performer who can put it over well.

One way of reminding the audience of the range of Burns's songs is to include a selection of airs to the songs as a solo instrumental item, perhaps while the guests assemble, during the service of coffee, or as an item between speeches.

I have already referred to the works of others (page 36) and I see no harm in these provided they do not mar the enjoyment of Burns's own writings. The only plea I would make is that they should be the work of men of worth and not trash written by poetasters who cannot match the Bard in quality of thought or writing.

Unfortunately many anniversary dinners are held at which the principal guest gives a splendid oration, only to find that, apart from a few Burns songs, no other reference is made to the Bard or his works. This is fine as a club evening, but it isn't a Burns Supper!

Poems or songs written by others about Burns sometimes appear on Burns Night Programmes. Usually these are the work of earnest folk who genuinely want to honour the Bard, but they fall so far short in quality that they would be better omitted. The fact that they are presented on Burns Night alongside those of Burns merely serves to underline their shallowness and poor craftsmanship. That kind of "work by others" can well be dispensed with on Burns Night.

Let all the guests participate in the fun of the evening by joining in the choruses of the songs or even by singing a few of the songs together. But if that is to be done, make it an official part of the proceedings, and have the words duplicated or printed so that nobody has to hum or worse still get the words wrong.

There is one song about Burns which most clubs consider a "must" for their programme — *The Star O' Robbie Burns*. The *Star* was written by James Thomson, first president of Hawick Burns Club, who was born at Bowden on the Borders in 1827 and who developed such a love of the Poet that he carried a tattered Kilmarnock edition of Burns's poems in his pocket while he herded cows as a boy. Thomson published a volume of poems, but it is *The Star* by which he is remembered. Music for the song is by James Booth.

## THE STAR O' ROBBIE BURNS
### Words by James Thomson     Music by James Booth

There is a star whose beaming ray
Is shed on ev'ry clime
It shines by night, it shines by day
And ne'er grows dim wi' time
It rose up on the banks of Ayr,
It shone on Doon's clear stream —
A hundred years are gane and mair,
Yet brighter grows it's beam.

*Chorus*    *Let kings and courtiers rise and fa',*
*This world has mony turns*
*But brightly beams aboon them a'*
*The star o' Robbie Burns*

Though he was but a ploughman lad
And wore the hodden grey,
Auld Scotland's sweetest bards were bred
Aneath a roof o' strae.
To sweep the strings o' Scotia's lyre
It needs nae classic lore;
It's mither wit an' native fire
That warms the bosom's core

*Chorus*

On fame's emblazon'd page enshrin'd
His name is foremost now,
And many a costly wreath's been twin'd
To grace his honest brow
And Scotland's heart expands wi' joy
Whene'er the day returns
That gave the world its peasant boy —
Immortal Robbie Burns

*Chorus*

THE TIME to bring the Anniversary celebrations to an end is while the company is asking for more songs, recitations and music. In that way a few may be tempted to open their copy of Burns's Poems when they get home and read some for themselves.

It may be that a dance is to follow, but some of the company will not be staying on for this, so the Chairman will have to wind up the formal part of the evening.

First he will call on an official of the Club to thank the speakers and performers formally and express the thanks of the Club to the Chairman and secretary or organiser of the Dinner, and others connected with the success of the evening.

A guest may respond very briefly — a few words only — to express the appreciation of his fellow guests for the happy evening.

The Chairman now calls on the company to sing *Auld Lang Syne.*

This song, more than any other, means Robert Burns to the world. It has been translated into dozens of languages and is sung round the world by people who have never heard of Burns. *Auld Lang Syne* is recognised universally as a song of warmly remembered friendship and as a song of parting, but in Scotland, especially on Burns Night it takes on far deeper meaning. To us it is a reminder of our our roots, of the land and traditions which made us what we are. When I wrote my *Portrait of the Burns Country* I quoted two verses of *Auld*

*Lang Syne* which refer to the companions running "about the braes" and paidling in the burn", and I commented, "Every man has his own vision of the scene which these two verses conjure up, but for me, the burn is the one which flows gently into the river Doon just below Minishant, and the braes are the Whinnie Knowe above the village. And I never read or sing these verses without feeling the warmth of childhood summers there more than a generation ago."

It is now nearly two generations since I played on the Whinnie Knowe and beside the burn, but the feeling which *Auld Lang Syne* generates never changes. Yet it is not mere nostalgia that the song evokes: in it Burns uses remembrance of times and places past to look forward to a future full of hope.

> And there's a hand, my trusty fiere!\*     \* companion
> And gie's a hand o' thine
> And we'll tak a right gude-willie waught,\*     \* drink
> For Auld lang syne.

The mechanics of singing *Auld Lang Syne* arouse as much passion in Scottish hearts as calling the British Isles *England* or putting sugar in your porridge. Scots complain bitterly about non Scots singing "zyne" when they mean "syne", yet one hears these selfsame complainers sing "for the sake of auld land syne" where Burns wrote simply "for auld lang syne", and they sing "we'll meet again some ither night" which are not the words which Burns wrote.

Is it asking too much of anyone who is devoting a whole evening to honouring the Poet at a Burns Supper to spend half an hour beforehand running through the words — even committing them to memory. Everybody *nearly* knows *Auld Lang Syne* — but as we used to say as children, "Nearly never kil't a man". Perhaps not, but it has certainly murdered *Auld Lang Syne* often enough.

Here is Burns's version of the song:

Should auld acquaintance be forgot
          And never brought to mind?
Should auld acquaintance be forgot
          And auld lang syne.

Chorus:
      For auld lang syne, my jo,
          For auld lang syne,
      We'll tak a cup o' kindness yet
          For auld lang syne.

And surely ye'll be your pint stowp!*      * tankard
          And surely i'll be mine!
And we'll tak a cup  o' kindness yet,
          For auld lang syne.

Chorus
      We twa hae run about the braes,
          And pou'd the gowans* fine;    * large daisies
      But we've wandered mony a weary fitt,
          Sin' auld lang syne.

Chorus
      We twa hae paidl'd in the burn,
          Frae morning sun till dine;*    * dinner-time
      But seas between us braid* hae roar'd    * broad
      Sin' auld lang syne.

Chorus
      And there's a hand, my trusty fiere!
          And gie's a hand o' thine!
And we'll tak a right gude willie-waught,
          For auld lang syne

For auld lang syne, my jo,
For auld lang syne,
We'll tak a cup o' kindness yet,
For auld lang syne.

he party's over — the last guest has left and the chairman and organiser are alone with their thoughts. Throughout the evening both will have been watching every detail of the proceedings (not worrying about things unnecessarily, but taking in every detail). Within themselves they will know whether the Dinner was a success or if certain aspects of it could be improved next year.

Naturally, they will discuss it with other people to find out their comments, but one thing they will never know. There is no way of finding out how many people went home inspired to open a copy of Burns and read it.

There is still work to be done by the organiser. Speakers and entertainers may have been thanked verbally, but they should each be sent a brief letter of thanks. No doubt they had a good dinner and enjoyed themselves, but they did give up their time to attend your Burns Supper, and the club is in their debt at least to the extent of a letter of thanks. It costs a speaker time and trouble to attend a dinner, so never take him for granted.

If the local newspapers have been unable to attend, a brief report should be sent to them quickly, and of course, if the club is in membership of the Burns Federation a report should be sent to the Editor of the *Chronicle*.

Give some thought to how this should be worded. "Mr. . . proposed an eloquent Immortal Memory" may be true, but it tells those who were not present absolutely nothing about the event. Some organisers spread themselves and still say nothing. So give details of the speaker clearly and concisely, add a paragraph about the content of his speech, perhaps even a short quotation.

Before you send it off read it, for goodness sake. After speaking at a Dinner once I was amused to read in the Burns Chronicle: "The Immortal Memory was proposed by Mr. Hugh Douglas, followed by some excellent speeches and entertainers." I am still trying to work our whether the secretary meant what he wrote.

A committee meeting is usually held soon after the Anniversary Dinner, not so much as an inquest as to capitalise on the enthusiasm generated by the Dinner to start work on the next one. This is the time to make reservations, find speakers and to engage singers for next year. It is also the time to plan the programme for the remainder of the year.

The Burns Supper is only a small part of the year's activities for many clubs, the focal point of a programme which keeps Burns's work fresh in the minds of members.

Burns was a convivial man who would relish regular friendly meetings with plenty of companionship and laughter. This, much more than the formal dinner would please him, so regular meetings with talks, readings and discussions are a good basis for the Burns year. Visiting speakers from other clubs are a good idea because they bring a fresh view on Burns and his works, and, of course, outings can be made to kindred clubs.

St. Andrews Night ought to be the other highlight of the year, and here Burns can be put into the context of Scottish literary achievement. By showing the works of others — the balladmakers, the "greats" of the 18th century, Scott, Stevenson, Buchan and the many fine modern poets of Scotland — Burns will be shown to have had unique talents which set him apart from all the others. It will also come clearly through that, contrary to what many south of the Border think, Scotland is not a one-author country. Her heritage is rich and deserves to be better appreciated. Burns ought to be used to display this and not merely to go over his own talents again and again without relating them to anything else.

Burns must also be the basis for looking to the future. The Bard himself was a farsighted man, and this is why the Federation encourages work among young people through talks to schools and projects and competitions among schoolchildren with appropriate prizes of Burns's works. Where there is an interested or co-operative headmaster this work is achieving much in promoting knowledge and interest. If there is no glowing spark in a school already, then it is up to the club to ignite one. Talk to the teachers, offer to come and speak about Burns to the children, invite the headmaster to be a guest to your Dinner, and keep in touch with him about your club activities.

Perhaps one way of arousing interest in the teachers is to show that Burns can help to create a wider interest in Scottish literature generally. Instead of a Burns competition run a general Scottish literature one, or one for writing in

Scottish dialect. Always think broadly when promoting Burns, and you will come close to the Poet's own objectives.

Because the focus of the Burns cult is the Poet's birthday, Burns tends to be thought of as a man of winter. Nothing could be further from the truth: Burns's health deteriorated as winter fastened her grip on the Scottish landscape and his spirits ebbed until he was a mere shadow of his real self.

Spring returned and the warming sun slowly restored his health and his spirits. In the bleak Scottish climate the process was a slow one, and he himself admitted that it was August before he was in song again. In 1796 the returning sun was too slow and Burns never recovered. He died in July.

At many places a ceremony is held to mark the Poet's death, usually with a wreath-laying, but at Ayr a service is held at Leglen Wood and a new dimension has been brought to the movement by an annual Burns Festival, held throughout the Burns Country, consisting of talks, concerts and other activities. It is right that a summer festival should be associated with the Poet who was so much a man of that season.

This broadening of the Burns cult can never overshadow the 25th January. Burns Night will always have a special meaning for Scots whether at home or in exile in some far part of the world. To non-Scots the Burns Supper may appear at best something faintly comic and at worst a hard-drinking, haggis-praising night which turns the Dr Jekyll in the Scot into a Mr Hyde. A few

Burns Suppers may deserve that description, but by and large the celebration is a serious one, to be taken earnestly even by those organisations which have no direct connection with Burns.

The Burns Supper means more to the Scot than any stranger can understand. A well-travelled Scot summed it all up to me in a letter recently: "It is when you are very far from home that a Burns Supper takes on a completely new form. One night in Melbourne many years ago, my father, a keen member of Melbourne Burns Club, brought home a starving man who had been working in the Outback for many months. We found out he was a Scot, called Tom Wilson, a weaver from Hawick, and having been fed and clothed Tom marched round the garden playing Common Riding songs on his bugle. Then out of his knapsack he took three books — a Bible, Lockhart's Life of Scott and Burns's Poems. With tears running down his cheeks he read his favourite, *The Cotter's Saturday Night.* My father's reward was to take Tom to the next Burns Supper where Tom was the star of the evening, next to Burns himself."

The 25th of January is the one day of the year when the Scot returns to his roots; when he takes stock of himself. It is only right that the focus of this re-dedication should be the man who, more than any other, helped Scotland to retain her nationhood, her heritage and her native tongue.

But Robert Burns no longer belongs to Scotland alone. He is a citizen of the whole world, a man who can express the feelings of all men and remind them of their finest qualities. He is the Poet who never lost sight of the brotherhood of man and he won't let us lose sight of it either.

Thus the Burns Supper has become more than a convivial gathering — convivial though it may be — It is a celebration with power to do immense good. Burns does not need the celebrations of each 25th of January to keep him alive: what he had to say and the way in which he expressed it are important enough to guarantee him immortality.

It is *we* who need Burns and the Burns Night celebration to remind us of all the good that is encapsulated in the Poet's works, and to live by the principles which he laid down.

## THE APT QUOTATION

Finding the right quotation to illustrate an aspect of Burns can be daunting for the beginner. It is impossible to plough through hundreds of poems in the faint hope of discovering a suitable one.

This list, although by no means complete, points to the poems to read on a variety of subjects likely to be of help to speakers at Burns Suppers.

## About his own life

There was a Lad
The Cotter's Saturday Night
To Willie Simpson
Epistles to Davie

## Satire on religion and the Church

The Holy Tulzie
Holy Willie's Prayer
The Holy Fair
The Ordination
The Kirk's Alarm
The Twa Herds

## Other Satires

Death and Doctor Hornbook
The Twa Dugs
Address to the Deil

## The Dignity and suffering of Man

Man was made to Mourn
On seeing a Wounded Hare
A Man's a Man for A' That
To a Mouse
The Twa Dugs

## Patriotism

Scots Wha Hae
Does Haughty Gaul Invasion Threat

## Jacobitism

A Highland Lad my love was born
Lines written at Stirling
  (Here Stewarts once in triumph reign'd)
The Bonnie Lass of Albanie
Up and Warn a' Willie
Hey Johnnie Cope
The White Cockade
  (My love was born in Aberdeen)
The Luvely Lass o' Inverness
Charlie he's my Darling

## Love

I'm o'er young to marry yet
A Rosebud by my early walk
Of a' the airts
O were I on Parnassus hill
Afton Water
The Lea Rig
O Whistle and I'll come to ye, my lad
My Love she's but a Lassie yet
John Anderson my Jo
Ye Banks and Braes o' Bonnie Doon
Ae Fond Kiss
Bonnie Wee Thing
Willie Wastle

## Drinking

Willie Brew'd a Peck o' Maut
The De'il's awa' wi' th' Exciseman
John Barleycorn
Scotch Drink

*Remembrance and Parting*

> Auld Lang Syne
> Ae Fond Kiss

*Some Useful Quotations which are hard to find unless you know your way around Burns's poetry and song.*

Then gently scan your brother man,
 Still gentler sister woman;
Tho' they may gang a kennin* wrang,   * little
 To step aside is human.
      (Address to the Unco Guid)

Auld Coila now may fidge fu' fain,*  * get excited
She's gotten Bardies o' her ain,
Chiels wha their chanters winna hain,*  * spare
 But tune their lays,
Till echoes a' resound again
 Her weel-sung praise.
      (To Willie Simpson)

O Death! the poor man's dearest friend,
 The kindest and the best!
Welcome the hour my aged limbs
 Are laid with thee at rest.
      (Man was made to Mourn)

The best-laid schemes o' mice and men
 Gang aft agley,*    * wrong
An' lea'e us nought but grief an' pain
 For promis'd joy.
      (To a Mouse)

Fortune! if thou'll but gie me still
Hale breeks,* a scone, an' whisky gill,  * trousers
An' rowth o' rhyme to rave at will,
 Tak' a' the rest.
      (Scotch Drink)

O wad some Power the giftie gie us
To see oursels as ithers see us!
It wad frae monie a blunder free us
        An' foolish notion.

(To a Louse)


Long may we live! Long may we love!
        And long may we be happy!!
And may we never want a glass,
        Well charged with generous Nappy!!*        * ale
        (To Clarinda: Fair Empress of the Poet's Soul)


But pleasures are like poppies spread,
You seize the flower, its bloom is shed;
Or like the snow falls in the river,
A moment white — then melts for ever;
Or like the borealis race,
That flit ere you can point their place;
Or like the rainbow's lovely form,
Evanishing amid the storm.

(Tam O' Shanter)


Nae man can tether time or tide.

(Tam O' Shanter)


Had we never lov'd sae kindly,
Had we never lov'd sae blindly,
Never met — or never parted,
We had ne'er been broken-hearted.

(Ae Fond Kiss)


Then let us pray that come it may,
        As come it will for a' that,
That sense and worth, o'er a' the earth,
        Shall bear the gree,* and a' that.    * win first place
                        (A Man's a Man for a' That)


The heart ay's the part ay,
That makes us right or wrang.

(Epistle to Davie)


I'm truly sorry man's dominion
Has broken Nature's social union.

(To a Mouse)

Man's inhumanity to man,
Makes countless thousands mourn!

(Man was Made to Mourn)


From scenes like these, old Scotia's grandeur springs,
    That makes her lov'd at home, rever'd abroad:
Princes and lords are but the breath of kings,
    'An honest man's the noble(st) work of God';

(The Cotter's Saturday Night)


Gie me ae spark o' Nature's fire,
That's a' the learning I desire.

(First Epistle to John Lapraik)


'The social, friendly, honest man,
    Whate'er he be,
'Tis he fulfils great Nature's plan,
    And none but he.'

(Second Epistle to John Lapraik)


There's nought but care on ev'ry han',
In ev'ry hour that passes, O:
What signifies the life o' man,
An' twere na for the lasses, O.

(Green Grow the Rashes, O)


Auld Nature swears, the lovely dears,
Her noblest work she classes, O;
Her 'prentice han' she tried on man,
An' then she made the lasses, O.

Green Grow the Rashes, O)


I wasna fou,* but just had plenty.                    * drunk

(Death and Dr. Hornbook)


Farewell to the Highlands, farewell to the North,
The birthplace of valour, the country of worth!
Wherever I wander, whever I rove,
The hills of the Highlands for ever I love.

(My Heart's in the Highlands)

If there's a hole in a' your coats,
    I rede you tent* it;                    * attend to
A chiel's amang you, takin' notes
    And, faith, he'll prent it.
            (On the late Captain Grose's Peregrinations
                                    thro' Scotland)

If there's another world, he lives in bliss;
If there is none, he made the best of this.
                    (Epitaph on William Muir)

Then at the balance let's be mute,
    We never can adjust it.
What's done we partly may compute,
    But know not what's resisted.
                    (Address to the Unco Guid)

But facts are chiels that winna ding,*    * won't be changed
    And downa* be disputed.                    * cannot
                                    (A Dream)

Some rhyme a neebour's name to lash;
Some rhyme (vain thought!) for needfu' cash;
Some rhyme to court the countra clash,*        * gossip
    An' raise a din:
For me, an aim I never fash;
    I rhyme for fun.
                    (Epistle to James Smith)

## BOOKS TO HELP YOU

### ON SPEAKING

Pan Guide to Public Speaking — Pan Books
Public Speaker's Treasure Chest — Thorsons Publishers
Treasury of Wit and Humour — Thorsons Publishers

# ON SCOTLAND, ITS HISTORY AND CULTURE

A short History of Scotland
    by R.L. Mackie — Penguin
The Lion in the North
    by John Prebble — Penguin
The Scots Kitchen
    by F. Marian McNeill — Blackie
A Taste of Scotland
    Fitzgibbon — Pan
Ena Baxter's Scots Cook Book
    Johnstone & Bacon

## ON THE BURNS COUNTRY

Portrait of the Burns Country
    by Hugh Douglas — Robert Hale
Ayrshire by John Strawhorn
    Ayrshire Archaeological and Natural History Society
Ayrshire at the time of Burns
    Ayrshire Archaeological and Natural History Society

## ON ROBERT BURNS

Life of Robert Burns
    by Catherine Carswell — Chatto & Windus
Robert Burns and His World
    by David Daiches — Thames and Hudson
Robert Burns. A Life
    by Hugh Douglas — Robert Hale
Robert Burns, the Man and His Work
    by Hans Hecht — Alloway Publishing
Robert Burns, The Man, His Work, The Legend
    by Maurice Lindsay — Robert Hale
The Burns Encyclopedia
    by Maurice Lindsay — Robert Hale
Life of Burns
    by J.G. Lockhart — J.M. Dent
The Burns Chronicle (Annual)
    Burns Federation

## BURNS' WORKS

Burns' Poems and Songs
    Edited by James Kinsley — Oxford University Press
The Letters of Burns — Edited by De Lancey Ferguson
    Oxford University Press
Selected Poems of Robert Burns
    Edited by David Daiches — Collins
Burns
    Penguin Poets — Penguin
Burns. A Study of the Poems and Songs
    by Thomas Crawford — The Mercat Press

## "THE DRAM"

HE DRAM has always played an important role in celebrating Burns Night. Just as we look to Burns to illuminate our spirit and remind us of our national heritage, so we take a dram to focus our attention on the present, bring the past more vividly to life and add a rosy glow to the future.

The whisky we drink now is, however, very different from that enjoyed by Burns — some of which may even have originated in the illicit stills which were the bane of his life and that of his fellow Excisemen.

In those early days 'uisge beatha' (the water of life which we know today as whisky) was distilled in Scotland by the local people for their own consumption. It would have been rough in comparison with the blends we enjoy today, little time being allowed for aging and scant consideration given to the fact that it was probably comparatively impure.

But it was a popular and heartwarming drink with the sturdy farming folk who took a jug of their own brew with them when visiting friends: this would be added to a communal container to be mixed with the whisky brought by other guests.

Although originally a Highland drink, by the time of the first Burns Suppers (in the early 1800's) the popularity of whisky had begun to spread south to be enjoyed by Scots throughout the land.

It was appropriate then, that another Ayrshire son, Johnnie Walker, should be among the first to popularise this wild spirit, first of all at home and later abroad.

John Walker opened a small grocery, wine and spirit shop in Kilmarnock in 1820. It was near the old Toll Gate, where merchants had to pay their taxes before they could leave the town, and close by the Town Hall: the window looked out onto the main thoroughfare, King Street, where the north/south coaches sped past.

The shop was in an ideal situation to catch the eye of the travelling merchants who had come to the town in search of carpets and textiles — items for which Kilmarnock was renowned in both Scotland and England.

In addition to gaining fame for printing the first edition of Burns's works, Kilmarnock was soon to become known for another commodity — Walker's Kilmarnock whisky. (In those days it was probably made from a mixture of pure Lowland malts which would have given it a very firm character, rather different from today's subtler blend of Highland and Lowland malt and grain whiskies.) The original success of John Walker was due in no small measure to the location of his premises. Kilmarnock was a thriving town at the very centre of activities in the industrial revolution, the early coaches stopped off there and when the railway came, it was on the main line to Glasgow.

In 1888 Alexander Walker's son — also called Alexander — joined the company and two years later a company office was opened in Sydney, Australia.

With demand for its products continuing to rise at an incredible rate, in 1893 the company acquired Cardow Distillery on Speyside, which remains an important part of its operations today.

With the turn of the century came new sales ideas and advertising techniques. Foremost amongst these was the introduction of the trade mark which has become so familiar around the world.

In 1908, Sir Alexander Walker decided to incorporate a portrait of his grandfather, founder of the firm, into the advertising scheme. He commissioned Tom Browne, a celebrated commercial artist of the time, to sketch a cheerful figure, complete with top hat, eyeglass and cane, stepping out with a purposeful stride. Sir Alexander's colleague, Lord Stevenson, later joint managing director, scribbled along the side of the page the catch-phrase that was to become so famous: "Johnnie Walker, born 1820 — still going strong".

This original sketch was miraculously rescued unharmed from Walker's premises which were bombed during World War II and it still remains a prized possession of the company today.

The name "Walker's Kilmarnock Whisky" was dropped and a new livery of Red and Black Labels set at a slant on the now famous square bottles was adopted, together with the Johnnie Walker striding figure trade mark. (The words and design were registered in 1910). These distinctive features have helped to gain an international identity for the company's blends of Scotch whisky and today the Johnnie Walker Scotch whisky blending and bottling operation is the largest in the world.

So, no matter where you may be on Burns Night, you can be sure of enjoying it that little bit more authentically with a glass of Johnnie Walker.

# LIST OF SUPPLIERS

**Y**ou may find some difficulty in obtaining the various ingredients you require for your Burns Supper locally. This depends, of course, on where you are celebrating Burns Night; in Scotland it is comparatively easy, but in darkest Cornwall, or California it may not be so simple.

To help you the following firms will be delighted to receive your enquiries and will make every endeavour to supply your needs, or advise you where their products can be obtained. Obviously it is to your advantage, as well as to the suppliers, if you place your orders well in advance so that despatch can be made at the right time. Most of these firms regularly supply throughout the U.K. and also have export departments.

One difficulty which can arise is over the exportation of Haggis. Some countries make it particularly difficult for haggis-makers to send haggis in for resale. In many cases the difficulties appear to be overcome by the organisers ordering for "own consumption" direct from the makers.

We would advise you to contact the haggis-maker of your choice and see what they recommend in your particular circumstances.

The information given here is accurate at the time of going to press, and will be updated in subsequent reprints.

## WHITE HEATHER SPRAYS

Scottish White Heather Farm
Toward, Dunoon, Argyll.
Telephone 036 987 237

## HAGGIS TRADITIONAL RECIPE

William W. Wales,
30 Orchard Street, Galston, Ayrshire, Scotland.
Telephone 0563 820483

## AWARD WINNING HAGGIS
### Traditional Recipe

John Henderson,
67 High Street, Kirkcaldy, Fife.
Telephone 0592 260980

## CANNED SCOTCH HAGGIS

Grant Bros. (Meat Canners) Ltd.,
Richmond Bridge, Galston, Ayrshire, Scotland.
Telephone 0563 820401    Telex 779775

## OATCAKES & BANNOCKS

Nairns
Wardieburn House, Edinburgh, EH5 2DL.
Telephone 031 551 1101

## ALL-BUTTER SHORTBREAD

Simmers
Wardieburn House, Edinburgh, EH5 2DL.
Telephone 031 551 1101

## GENUINE SCOTTISH LACE DESIGN TABLECLOTH
"Made in Burns Country"

Bonfab
West Donington Street, Darvel, Ayrshire.
Telephone 0560 20453    Telex 778026